CONTENTS

INTRODUCTION

The making of this book and video clips has been a fun yet demanding journey for me. Many books give some facts, but I wanted to create a book that teaches the developing saxophonist *how* to learn. Writing original music, listening, exploring, and trial and error are some of the techniques threaded throughout this book. Also, I included many of the techniques in this book (as opposed to other ones) because they're topics of interest that come up when I present clinics and master classes. These concepts will keep you learning, maturing, and mastering the saxophone in modern times, and for many years to come. I feel that you have to see what works best for you as an individual saxophonist in order to develop your own sound and voice, so that you can keep the role of the saxophone growing.

It has been said that art is the highest form of intelligence. It has also been said that there are three levels of development needed to be considered an artist:

1. **Imitation.** By imitating your favorite players that came before you, you'll get your foundation.
2. **Emulation.** Once you have listened to and imitated your favorite players diligently, then you begin to have your own ideas, sounds, vocabulary, compositions, etc. and begin to bring something special to the music.
3. **Innovation.** The distinct honor of influencing future generations of musicians is bestowed upon those rare saxophonists who become innovators and trendsetters.

It doesn't matter if you're playing, classical, jazz, reggae, or Celtic because these techniques will help you improve your sound, time, facility, ears, and control in order to make you a better player in all styles of music. Consider this a workbook and write down honest answers to the questions I ask – as well as any other thoughts, ideas, or discoveries you come up with along the way.

Also refer to the companion video clips. The "Quick Tips" section was devised to help with concepts that are difficult for most developing saxophonists. The "You Are in the Band" part was designed to create a jam session vibe where you'll jump in and out musically, much like what might happen while jamming live at a jazz club. I realize that many saxophonists using this book may not have jazz as their main musical focus, but I think that's even more reason to get acquainted with improvising. Improvisation is a huge key to success for most instrumentalists in current times. Bach and Mozart were great improvisers, so give it your best effort!

IT'S ALL ABOUT TIME

Having a great sense of time is crucial for making music. Whether you're playing in a saxophone quartet, orchestra, jazz big band, or funk band, having good time is essential. We wanted to start this book off with techniques and concepts addressing time because I feel it is often overlooked when teaching or learning the saxophone. Most of my favorite saxoph*onists a*lso play some drums. Time is not as easy to teach as some other concepts; time has to be *felt*. Even though most rhythms have a definite value, much in the way that 2 + 2 = 4, you'll find that when playing with a band or ensemble there are often slight *fluctuations or negotiations*. Saxophonists have to make sure their time is solid so that they don't need to rely upon a metronome or simply follow other musicians with good time. You should practice with a metronome often so you can keep your time *in check*.

Here is a list of questions for you to review and answer. There are no wrong answers, but answer them honestly, so you can assess your strengths and weaknesses.

- Do you feel like you rush or push your phrases when in an ensemble?
- Do you feel like you're behind or drag your phrases when in an ensemble?
- Do you feel like you're always perfectly in time when practicing to a metronome?
- Do you speed up when coming up to a difficult phrase?
- Do you slow down when coming up to a difficult phrase?
- Do you know all your scales?
- Do you know all your arpeggios?
- Can you count out and clap any rhythm you see written down?
- When improvising, can you start your phase at any rhythmic subdivision within the bar that you hear/choose?
- When improvising, can you end your phase at any rhythmic subdivision within the bar that you hear/choose?
- Can you change the rhythmic values of your phrases whenever you want – like eighth notes becoming triplets, for example?
- Can you double-time a phrase whenever you want?

Great saxophonists have mastery of all these techniques. Playing with first-rate musicians that inspire you to learn and grow as a player is important. Here are some things you can practice and work with that will improve your sense of time and the way you feel the pulse, so you will feel comfortable in any musical setting.

One-Note Groove

Feeling the time and/or pulse in the music you perform is crucial. I think the best way to begin improving and expanding the way you *feel the pulse* is to start simple. A fun and important example of what I'll call "one-note groove" is Stan Getz's version of the song "One Note Samba" by Antonio Carlos Jobim. Although the bulk of the melody is only one note, this recording received a huge amount of commercial and critical success. It's a prime example of how a musician with great groove and varied rhythm can make one note sound exciting to the audience.

Another example that comes to mind is the playing of bassist Bootsy Collins from the band Parliament Funkadelic. Bootsy keeps his bass lines simple and often leaves a lot of space. He almost always plays the root or 5th of the chord on the downbeat and then varies his lines on beats 2, 3, and 4 when in 4/4 time. Millions of people have heard and loved his playing; it's *simple* and great at the same time!

Can you please write a couple of eight-bar melodies that are only one note (like D for example), yet have a great deal of rhythmic interest?

Melody #1

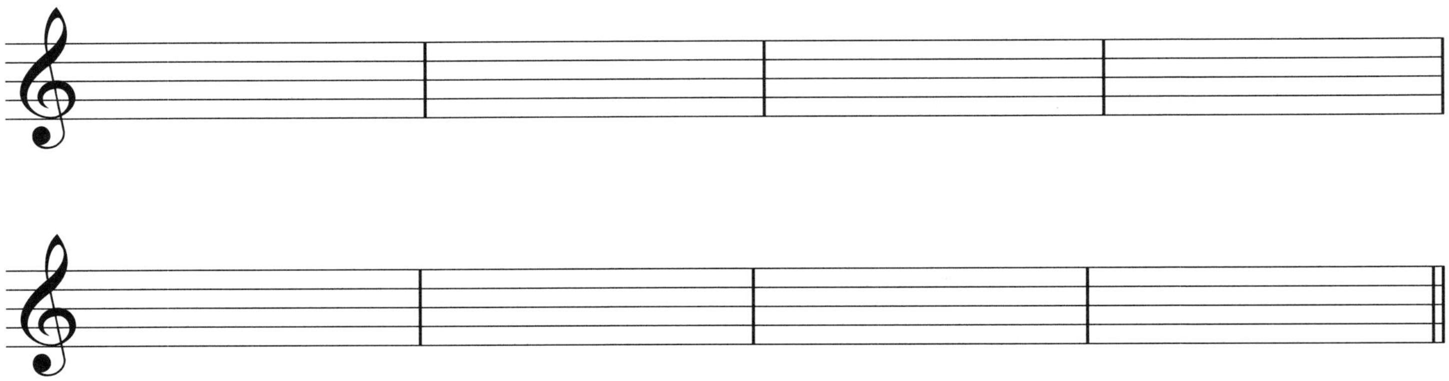

Melody #2

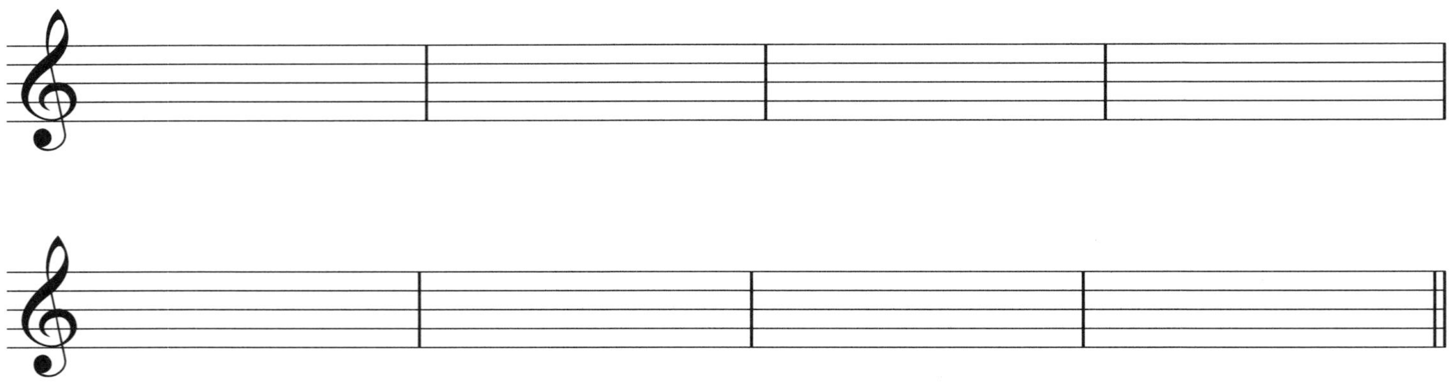

I have some fun examples here for you to play through. Feel free to write them out into different keys, too.

4/4 Time Study

4/4 Etude

On the One

More 4/4

3/4 Time Study

3/4 Etude

7/4 Time Study

7/4 Etude

How Do You Feel the Pulse?

After playing through these examples for a while, try experimenting with them in order to add new dimensions to the way you feel the pulse, time, and groove. Be sure to compose some of your own examples as well.

1. In 4/4 examples, try emphasizing beats 1 and 3 and then try emphasizing beats 2 and 4. What feels more natural for you? For just about all jazz and pop music, emphasis on 2 and 4 is crucial for the pulse of the music.
2. In 3/4 examples, try emphasizing beats 1, 2, and 3, then beats 1 and 3, and then just beat 1. Many pieces written in 3/4 – especially waltzes, which have a dance/swagger about them – become lethargic sounding if all three beats in the measure are emphasized. Emphasizing the downbeat – but not beats 2 and 3 – is a great way to give the music some flow and momentum.
3. For music that is in 7/4, first try emphasizing the downbeat. Then try subdividing the seven-beat measures into 1, 2, 3, 1, 2, 3, 4 and emphasizing the 1 each time. Then try subdividing the seven-beat measures in to 1, 2, 3, 1, 2, 1, 2 and emphasizing the 1 each time. Then try subdividing the measures into 1, 2, 1, 2, 3, 1, 2 and so on. What sounds best to you? Exploring the many possibilities will greatly expand your concept of time, phrasing, and groove.

Are You a Leader or a Follower?

When playing in an ensemble, the next important question to ask yourself is: Do you feel you're *leading* your section, are you perfectly *in synch* with your section, or are you a little nervous/tentative and therefore *following* the musicians in your section? Practicing the examples just discussed will add a great deal of knowledge and confidence to your playing so you won't be nervous and drag the time down or have flam/unclean entrances. You want to make sure your time is *right there* with everyone in your section, not pushing nor dragging.

Are Metronomes Good or Bad?

I've heard some great saxophonists say metronomes are critical to developing good time. I've heard other saxophonists say metronomes are bad for developing time because players become dependent on following the metronome instead of developing their own internal sense of time. So let me ask you what you think: Are metronomes good or bad? Yes? No? Why?

My favorite thing about a good metronome is that it doesn't lie. If you can't play a piece of music to a metronome, then working on your internal time, as well making sure you execute the music well, is crucial. My least favorite thing about using a metronome is that it doesn't allow some musicians to develop a strong internal pulse, since they tend to follow the metronome instead of *internalizing* the time feel. In order to get the best of both worlds, I suggest you practice regularly and diligently with a metronome, but also make sure to spend time practicing without it.

To assess your time, try recording your practice sessions. First, start the practice material with the metronome on. Then try the same material without the metronome. Listen to the recording and be your own worst critic. Do you hear more fluctuations in time and pulse on the recorded version without the metronome? If both versions sound the same, then your time is in pretty good shape. If there are fluctuations, then you need to focus on the metronome and continue to use it during your practice sessions to keep you in check.

How to Practice with a Metronome, Including Sight Reading

A lot of people practice with the metronome sounding on every beat. That is a bad idea, unless you're a beginning saxophonist. When you first start playing, having the metronome set on every beat is okay, but your goal should be to get away from this as soon as possible. If you're in 4/4 time, try setting the metronome to sound only on beats 2 and 4. If you're in 3/4 time, try making the metronome sound only on beat 1. Then have it sound only on beat 2. Then have it sound only on beat 3. Is one easier for you? Does one sound better than another?

Pick some phrases or write your own that are two to four measures long. Next, set the metronome to sound only on 2 and 4. Play each phrase twice at regular tempo then twice at double-time tempo. This is a great way to become comfortable with double-time transitions so you can begin incorporating them into your improvised solos. The metronome is an important tool for getting accustomed with single-time to *double-time* transitions, as well as double-time to *single-time* transitions.

It's extremely helpful to use a metronome while sight reading. When sight reading, you're trying to play the music accurately while simultaneously looking ahead so the music doesn't take you by surprise. Using a car analogy, if you're going 40 mph and look ahead a short distance, you'll likely hit pot holes and other road hazards that you could've easily avoided if you simply looked farther ahead. Similarly, if you're driving at a high speed and leave only a small space between your car and one in front of you, you'll potentially cause an accident that could have been avoided if you left more space between the two cars. Using this idea when it comes to sight reading, train yourself to look as far ahead as possible to avoid any trouble spots. At first, you might be able to look only a beat ahead. If you keep pushing yourself, soon you'll be looking at the next full bar. Eventually, you should be able to comfortably scan a few bars ahead while playing the music accurately in time with the ensemble.

Make sure you set the metronome *slower* than where you feel you can accurately play the piece. If you set the metronome too fast and have to stutter, you'll develop bad habits. The time must remain constant; it keeps marching on whether you execute the notes properly or not. If you set the metronome slightly slower than the tempo at which you can properly read a piece, it'll give your eyes a chance to start scanning the music ahead, instead of barely keeping up and making mistakes.

DEVELOPING YOUR SOUND

Developing a saxophone sound *you* like is the goal of this chapter. The first piece of advice is to listen, listen, and then listen some more. Listening to your favorite players, internalizing the nuances of their sound and style, and then combining that with *your* tastes, preferences, and original compositions is what will take you far as a musician and artist.

If your goal is to have a quality sound for ensemble playing, that's great, because these techniques will definitely help. Nothing would make me happier than to know that fellow saxophonists used these ideas to become successful soloists and recording artists. To be an artist, you ultimately need to bring something unique to the music; this distinction will be the reason people want to hear or hire *you* as opposed to another musician. Is your sound lush and pretty, perfect for a film score? Is your sound bold and brash, perfect for a rock band? Does it have soul and swagger, perfect for a Top 40 R&B track?

If you do a blindfold test, can you sonically tell the difference between Dexter Gordon, John Coltrane, David Sanborn, and Fred Hemke? They are all master saxophonists with distinctive styles. Even though Hemke was Sanborn's saxophone teacher, they sound quite different. You should go for what you're hearing and experiment from there. This chapter will feature a lot of techniques for you to explore, especially throat shapes or vowel shapes that are so important but rarely discussed. Everyone talks about embouchure because it is easy to see; you can look in the mirror and adjust. Unfortunately, you can't see the inside of your body while you're playing, so throat shapes are not as easy to address.

Have fun playing, developing, and trying out the concepts in this chapter, and most importantly, don't let anyone tell you how you should sound or improvise. Don't let anyone put boundaries on your artistic creativity. If a producer hires you for an eight-bar solo and says, "I want you to sound like Stan Getz," then you should probably give the producer what he or she is looking for if you want to be hired again. It is vital to know what all famous saxophonists sound like, but when it comes to *your* sound and art, follow your heart and don't let people tell you how to sound. Older players criticized Charlie Parker and John Coltrane when they were starting out because they sounded *different*. I would hate to think of what life would be like if Parker or Coltrane hadn't pushed on; so much of my favorite, most inspiring music would not have been made.

I think my favorite Frank Zappa quote applies to this: "Don't stop and keep going."

Embouchure

Here are some tips to form a quality embouchure. As you'll see, I'll talk about embouchure a few times in this book. First, I have a question: Can you look at some videos of a few of your favorite players and give me a few visual descriptions of what their mouth and embouchure look like?

____

____

____

Many great players have different types of embouchures, so it's vital that you find what works for you. For example, Dexter Gordon has a different embouchure than Eugene Rousseau. The embouchure that produces a quality sound with good intonation for *you* is what's important. Everyone's body is different, so some experimenting will be necessary – in addition to practicing in front of a mirror so you can *see* what you're doing. Let's start here:

- Cover your bottom teeth with your lower lip. The lower lip acts as a cushion for the reed to rest and vibrate, so the lower lip should not be drawn too tight.
- Your top teeth rest on the mouthpiece. The pressure around the mouthpiece should be enough that no air leaks, but it should feel natural and not too tight – no tensing or pinching. The reed needs to accept comfortably air and vibrate to get a good sound.
- The cheeks of your face shouldn't be drawn tight nor puffed. Your throat needs to be rather open and flexible, much as if you're singing or saying the vowel sound "ah."

Embouchure

Reed Placement and Strength

A few thoughts on reeds:

- Medium-strength reeds work best for about 95 percent of saxophonists.
- If the reed is a little too bright or soft, try moving the tip of the reed so it's a little bit above the tip of the mouthpiece.
- Reeds that play great at loud volumes but not at soft volumes are generally a little stiff. Try adjusting it so the tip of the reed is just below the tip of the mouthpiece.
- When a reed is the perfect strength for you, it should play great when its tip and the mouthpiece tip are perfectly even.
- Make sure the reed is sealing on the mouthpiece and that the ligature is the proper size so it can be fastened reasonably tight.
- Take a look at these three important parts of the reed: tip, heart, and vamp.

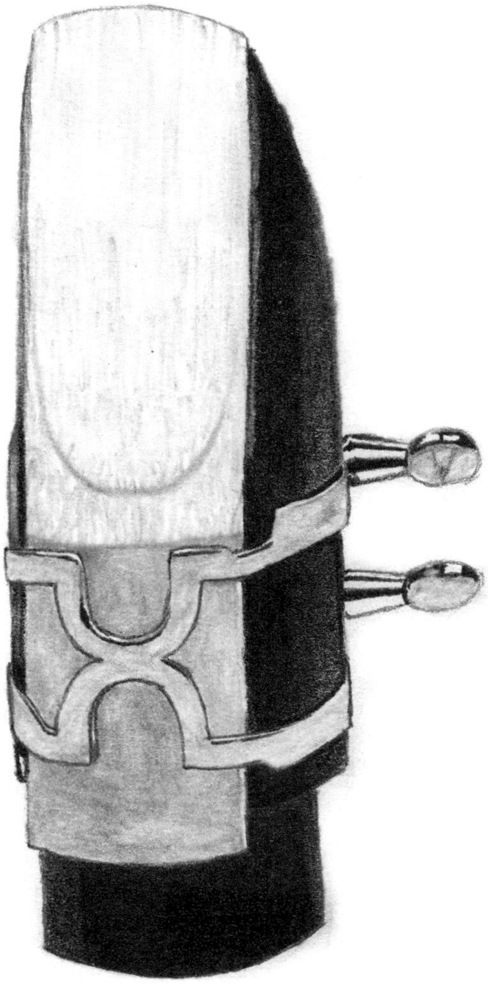

Reed Placement

Neck Position

The position of the saxophone neck should not be adjusted too far to the left or right. The position of *your* neck should be reasonably tall and not slouched, so that it is open enough to accommodate the air. Also, your neck needs to be flexible so that it can form the different vowel shapes (A, E, I, O, U), allowing you to have control over your sound production. (See page 12 for vowel illustrations.)

Air Stream

Your air stream is greatly affected by your throat and tongue. Your tongue should lie lower in your mouth and your throat should be reasonably open. I believe the "ah" vowel sound and throat shape best gets players going in the right direction. After you're comfortable with the "ah" shape and the sound it's helping you create on the saxophone, experiment with the other vowel shapes.

Resistance

Resistance is a necessary evil. You need some resistance to shape the sound and have something in which to help gauge your airstream, but too much is bad. Also, too much resistance from a small-sized mouthpiece and hard reed can cause physical problems. I definitely recommend starting on a medium-sized mouthpiece and medium-strength reed, and then experimenting from there.

Breathing

Breathing is important. You need to learn to create the largest possible inner chest cavity so your lungs can expand and take in as much air as possible. Good posture is also crucial. If sitting, your back should be straight and not resting on the back of the chair. When putting air into the saxophone, you need a controlled "column" or "cylinder" of air. If you visualize a round shape as your diaphragm is pushing, over time you'll have a lot more control, especially at soft volumes. If your outward breath is not round, you might start pinching in your embouchure to over-compensate, which makes the pitch sharp and the tone thin.

Breathing

Long Tones

Long tones are the best way to get your breathing and air stream in good shape. Play a chromatic scale and hold each note as long as you can. Then play it again, this time with each note *starting soft* and ending loud. Next, play it with each note *starting loud* and ending soft. Do this for a few months and your embouchure, air stream, and breathing will really come together nicely.

Long Tones

Shoulder Shrugs

I will mention the dreaded "shoulder shrugs" again later, but it's important to bring up the subject now. Make sure you practice your breathing and long tones in front of the mirror. Don't let your shoulders raise or shrug when you breathe in, because that means you're pinching and tightening instead of relaxing. This will mean a decrease in air intake/output, and intonation issues usually result as well.

Shoulder Shrugs

Where Do Your Teeth Hit the Mouthpiece?

Examine where your top teeth hit the mouthpiece. Some saxophonists have their teeth too far in or too far out. You must have your teeth far enough on the mouthpiece that a seal is made. Generally speaking, putting your teeth halfway on the "beak" of the mouthpiece is a good starting place. Everyone's body and mouthpieces vary, so you can adjust and experiment from there to see what works best for *you*.

Mouthpiece

Mouthpiece Position and Tuning

The position of your mouthpiece should be comfortable, not turned up on either side. Don't move your mouth for tuning purposes. Make the adjustments between the mouthpiece and the saxophone neck for tuning. If you're *flat*, move the mouthpiece *in* on the neck. If you're *sharp*, move the mouthpiece *out*. If you make adjustments between your mouth and the mouthpiece, your embouchure will suffer. It's vital that you follow these rules in order to keep your embouchure flexible.

HIGH NOTES

So you want to play some impressive, show-stopping high notes, right? The following tips will help you work *smarter*, not harder, so you can incorporate the altissimo (upper octave) notes of the saxophone into your vocabulary quickly.

Every modern player needs to have the ability to utilize the altissimo notes of the saxophone. This wasn't as important years back; in fact, legends like Charlie Parker rarely used it. Over time, the role of the saxophone has changed. In current settings, saxophonists are often expected to perform with electric guitars, DJs, etc., so having control over the entire range of the saxophone is essential. Since the 1970s, when saxophonists like Mike Brecker and David Sanborn transformed our beloved instrument into a pop, rock, and R&B mainstay, properly utilizing the altissimo notes has become a necessary skill. In classical music, the altissimo was at one time considered an "extended technique," but in modern times mastery of the altissimo range is considered a must. Some might say the altissimo range is a necessary evil due to the difficult learning process required to make these high notes sound like a controlled and natural part of the saxophone's voice. Without proper control and technique, these high tones can sound like a screechy annoyance.

Have no fear: This chapter will explain the Do's and Don'ts of the altissimo range and thus speed up the learning process. Have patience, because it's important to learn these skills right the first time. The concepts I'm discussing will save you time and energy. These concepts will also eliminate the possibility of developing bad habits and the frustration that comes with having to unlearn them.

Control

First, let's discuss important **Don'ts**.

1. **Don't pinch the reed or use excessive lip/embouchure pressure.** It is important to keep your embouchure flexible. I have seen students put their teeth on the reed itself and bite down to produce horribly annoying high-pitched sounds. I wouldn't even call them "notes" because they're not an exact pitch. What's worse, this will crack your reed and keep you from being able to develop solid control.
2. **Don't shrug your shoulders or tighten/constrict your air flow.** Many players do this in a fierce struggle to get these challenging notes out of the saxophone. Some players over-compensate and manage to squeeze out a few high notes here and there. While it might seem like that is working at first, there is no solid control of the notes. The goal is to be able to strongly play high notes with 100 percent accuracy and precision. Any shortcuts will be a catalyst for developing bad habits.

With that out of the way, let's talk about the **Do's**.

See the fingering chart on page 11. These are the fingerings I use and I know they work great. There are many altissimo fingering options so experiment to discover what works for you. Since the altissimo works off the overtone series, see the diagram of the notes of the overtone series (page 11). This is important because altissimo notes don't naturally jump out of the saxophone as easily as the notes in its normal range. A combination of embouchure, air stream, and ear training are crucial for successful results.

1. **Make sure you can hear in your head the note you want to play.** Now that you have familiarized yourself with the overtone series, you can appreciate that to hear and visualize the note you want to play is crucial. As I mentioned, altissimo notes do not pop out as easily as the notes in the normal range of the saxophone. They are harmonics built off the

overtone series and, as you have surely noticed, some fingerings are the same (G and D, for example), so ear training is important. The ability to hear the desired note in your head is the key to synching your airstream, embouchure, and body for desired results.

2. **Your embouchure and body must be relaxed.** I suggest practicing in front of a mirror to make sure you're not over-compensating. Your embouchure should be flexible and not pinched in any way. Watching your embouchure in the mirror should help you avoid any bad habits. If your embouchure is flexible, you can best control the attack, release, vibrato, etc. of the notes. Also avoid having your bottom lip overly tucked in or out. Your bottom teeth should press against your lip, so that a seal is created between your lip (embouchure), reed, and mouth piece. This is crucial for maximizing air flow. A solid air stream is needed for these high notes.
3. **Much like a singer focuses on vowels, so should a saxophone player.** I am shocked that people rarely discuss the similarities between singers and saxophonists. Singing A-E-I-O-U results in different shapes in your throat and thus a change in air stream. Remember: The saxophone is an extension of your body. The key to full, controlled high notes is being able to control your air stream. Think of a garden hose. If you put your thumb over the end of the hose, the intensity/velocity of the water flow increases. The water shoots out, but the amount of water coming though the hose doesn't change. By using the different vowel shapes in your throat, you can sculpt your body to change your air stream/flow. The result is more possibilities without having to exert more physical energy. Work smarter, not harder! In this way, you can efficiently maximize your air and play day after day in high-energy settings without getting fatigued. Spend time getting accustomed to how the different vowel shapes affect your sound and the notes themselves. A relaxed body with a supported air stream and the E vowel shape/throat concentration is the most effective way to effortlessly get the altissimo range to sing out. The vowel shape is crucial to shaping your sound, so spend time exploring this (and check out the online video clips to hear demonstrations). Some basic warm-ups like singing the vowels in a triad of scales can also be effective in synching your mind/ear/body.

Once your body, mind, and saxophone work in synch, you can develop total control of the instrument, ensuring that you can execute your desired note choices every time and achieve the ultimate goal of artistic expression.

Overtone Series

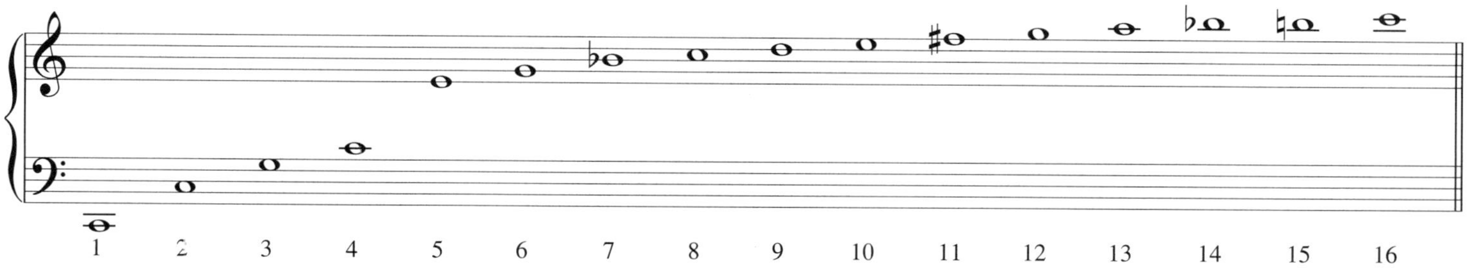

Altissimo Fingering Chart

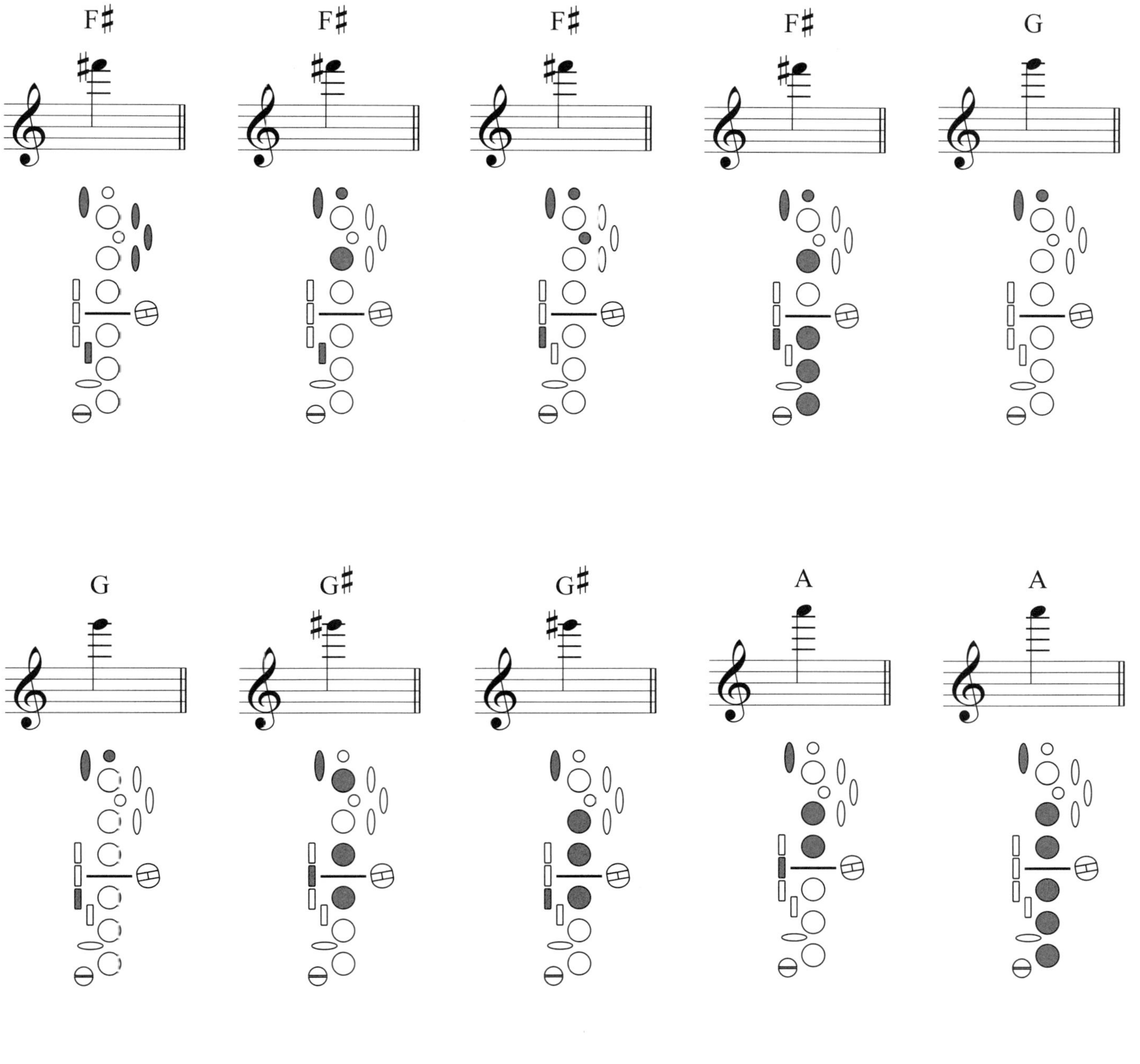

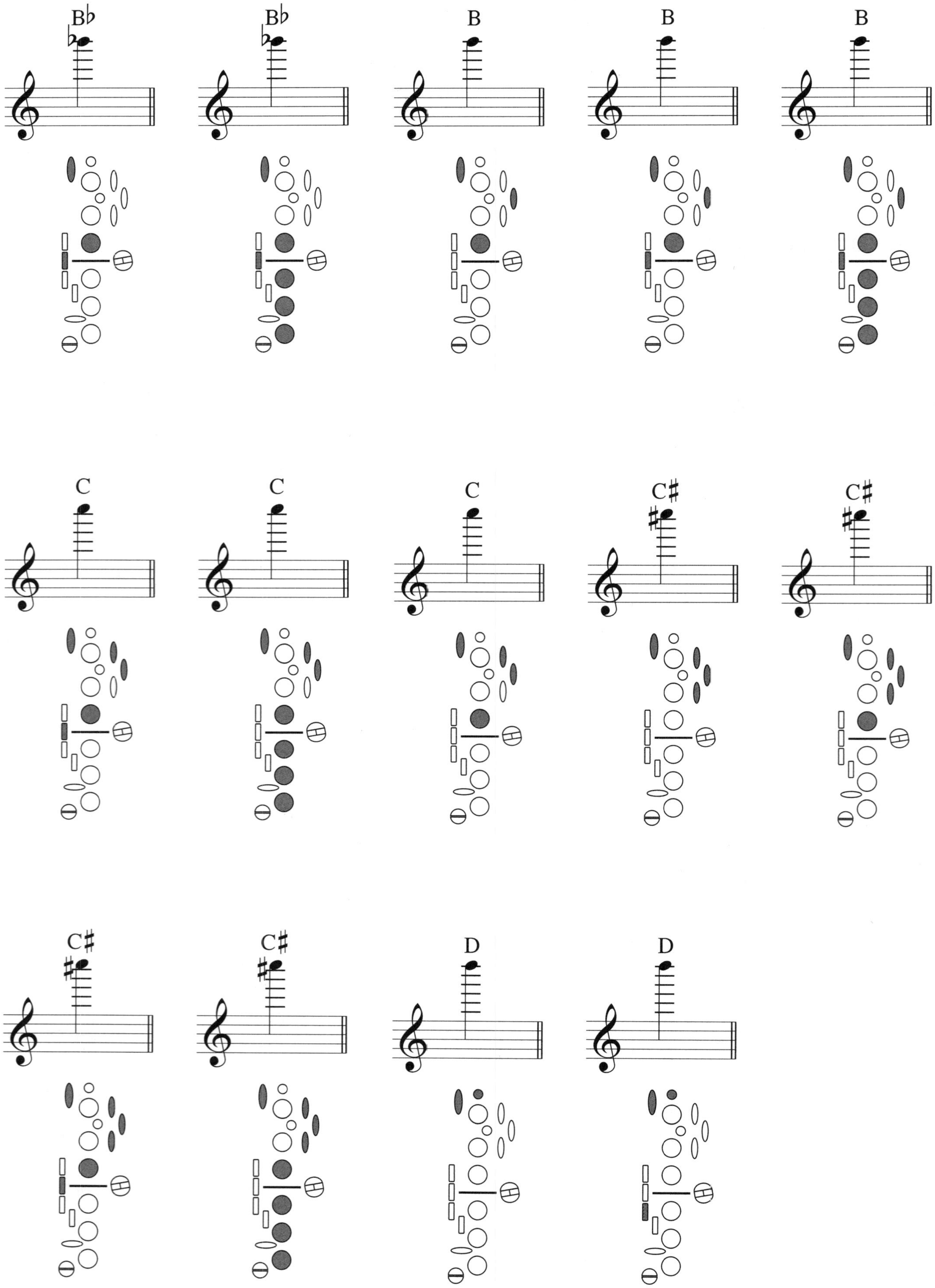
B♭
B♭
B
B
B
C
C
C
C♯
C♯
C♯
C♯
D
D

A, E, I, O, U Vowel Throat Positions

A

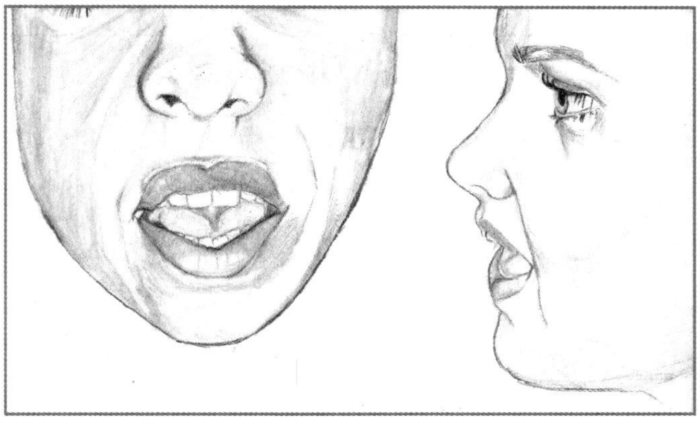

E

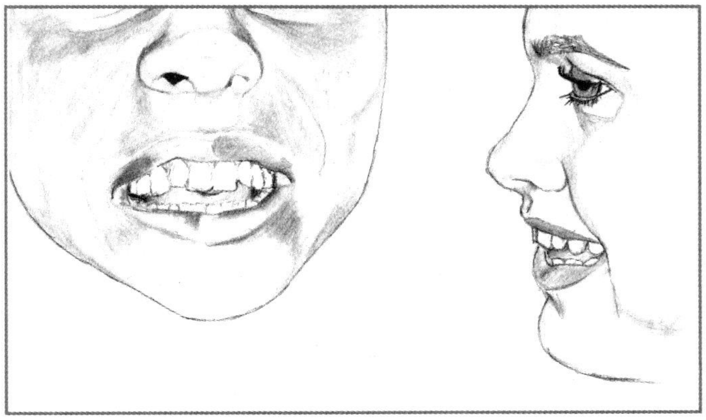

I

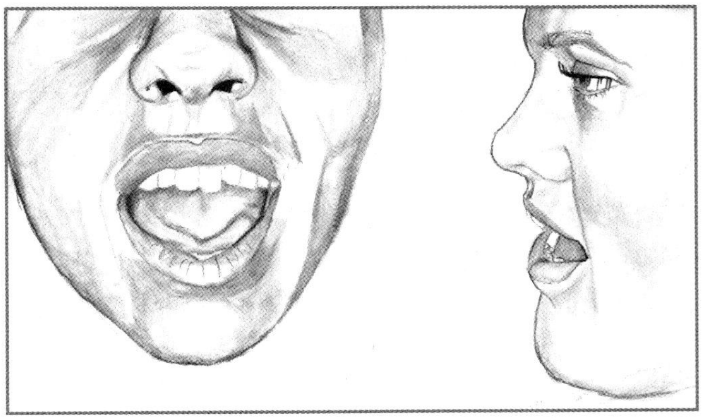

O

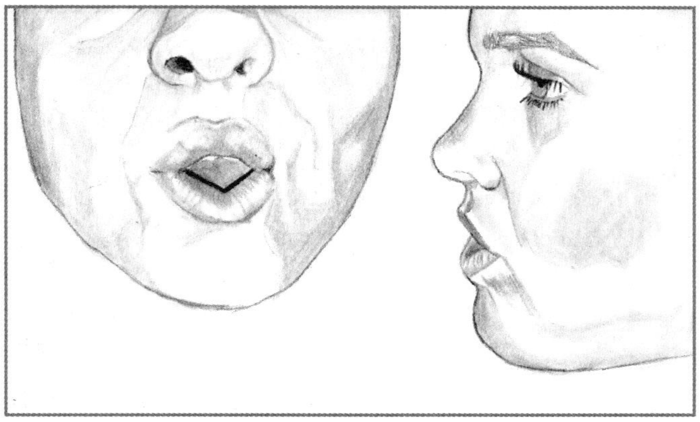

U

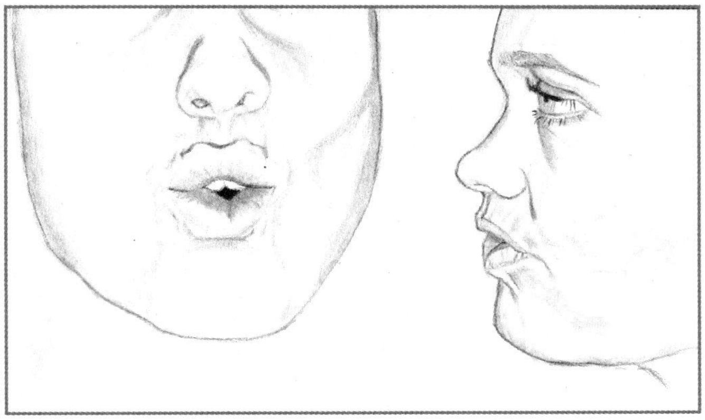

EXTENDED SOUND TECHNIQUES

Let's discuss some ways to vary the sound quality and/or timbre of the saxophone. When I first started playing, some teachers referred to these concepts as "extended techniques" or "extended sound techniques" because they push the sonic boundaries well beyond the standard or traditional "clean" sound most people associate with the saxophone.

Contemporary classical saxophonists like Siguard Rascher began introducing harmonics and multi-phonics into their performances in the 1930s. Harmonics have always been important to saxophonists for tuning and sound production, but incorporating harmonics and multi-phonics into performances made them some of the first extended techniques. In 1959, John Coltrane's "Harmonique" was met with mixed reaction as it was the first jazz recording to feature harmonics and multi-phonics as melodic material. Many people felt it was unpleasant to hear and too avant-garde. Others loved its sonic complexity and welcomed this departure from traditional jazz, which they felt was becoming stale and tired. In modern times, the techniques in this chapter should be explored by all saxophonists wishing to perform classical, jazz, rock, pop, dance, etc. with a contemporary approach.

Split-Tones

What is your definition of split-tones? I grew up listening to David Sanborn's playing, and loved it since he'd mastered the art of utilizing split-tones to accent his phrases. My definition of split-tones is "accelerating your airflow so that the desired note does not change pitch, rather its timbre changes because more harmonics are added to the desired note." Others might have a slightly different definition, but the objective is to make the desired pitch have a dirtier, grittier, and slightly overblown sound. While split-tones came easily for me on the alto and baritone saxophones, it took me years of additional practice before I was proficient on soprano and tenor.

It's not unusual to receive 20 or 30 emails a week from saxophonists asking me for split-tone tips, so I will address the topic here. I started calling this extended technique "split-tones" about 25 years ago. Later, I did a mini-clinic for the Rico Reeds/D'Addario website on the subject and was shocked by the large number of saxophonists who wrote to thank me. I was also surprised to get emails from people confusing split-tones with the R&B-style "growl" that I will discuss later.

Firstly, split-tones are created by *accelerating* your air; this doesn't mean blowing harder like many uninformed saxophonists think. Rather, it's about focusing your air. Consider this analogy: When helping my Dad wash the car as a kid, our hose didn't have a spray nozzle, so water would flow slowly to the ground. By placing his thumb at the end of the hose, my Dad could direct and intensify the water flow so that he could spray down the car. As a five-year-old kid this seemed like magic, as if someone must be turning up the water pressure, right? No, it was exactly the same amount of water coming out. When applied to the saxophone, players must use roughly the same amount of airflow but with more speed and focus; we don't want more air because we don't want to over-blow the note and make the reed shut down. I recommend the ee vowel throat shape for most notes and sometimes the A vowel shape.

Here are the throat/vowel shapes that I use for split-tones:

- G with octave key: ay vowel
- G♯ with octave key: ay vowel
- A with octave key: ee vowel
- A♯: ee vowel
- B: ee vowel
- C: ee vowel
- C♯: ah vowel
- D palm key: ay vowel
- D♯ palm: ay vowel
- E palm: ee vowel

There is a certain amount of "channeling" the overtone series that needs to take place. Also note that soft or hard reeds will keep split-tones from taking place; medium-strength reeds are best for split-tones. Large-chambered, old-school mouthpieces with smaller tip openings don't usually allow for split-tones. I say *usually* because everyone's body and mouth shape are different, so anything is possible. I love my JodyJazz mouthpiece because it's great for producing a fast airstream, yet I once played a 1960s Otto Link Slant Signature that easily produced a fast air stream and split-tones, even though it had a large chamber.

So, explore and experiment! If something works well for you, you'll know rather quickly, because it will feel comfortable and will allow you to fine-tune things from there.

Split-Tones

Sub-Tones

What is your favorite Dexter Gordon recording?

What is a sub-tone?

Dexter Gordon is my favorite sub-tone master. He could make the lowest notes of the saxophone sound full, round, airy, and nostalgic all at the same time. Sub-tones are when we play the lowest notes with a widened, slower air stream so that the notes don't sound harsh or abrasive. The same amount of air is used to play sub-tone low notes as it is to play regular low notes. For me, the best throat shapes to use are the oh and oo vowel shapes. The oo sounds like saying the word "sue" and produces the best results for me.

Sub-Tones

Bends à la Brecker (Brecker Bends)

What is your favorite recording by Michael Brecker?

Michael Brecker was a true voice and master of the saxophone. Randy Brecker has been an amazing mentor/friend/bandmate to me for 20 years. I feel fortunate to have learned so much from both of them. I would like to share this tidbit that I learned from Michael, which I am going to call the "Brecker Bends" for the sake of this book. The concept is to use only your lip/embouchure to produce a note a whole step below the note you're playing. For instance, play A with the octave key and then bend the note down to G and back up to A. The object is to keep the note centered and rich so that you feel the core of the note. It should almost sound like you actually played/fingered the note a whole step below and then fingered/played the original pitch. I feel the oo vowel shape (as heard in the word "sue") or the ay and/or ah vowel shape (as in "law") works best for the Brecker Bends. Again, try all the shapes and see if you discover something new for yourself! Refer to the Quick Tip in the online video.

Vowels

The R&B Growl

Do you know who King Curtis is? What about Junior Walker?

At a recent clinic, I asked the audience these two questions. Of the 400-plus saxophonists in the audience, only three hands went up. I felt truly sad because these two saxophonists have been so influential in the rock and R&B world; it seems to me that every saxophonist, regardless of preferred musical genre, should know Junior Walker and King Curtis! If you already know their music then great, but if not, please look them up! The R&B growl pioneered by saxophonists King Curtis, Junior Walker, Jimmy Forrest, and Louis Jordan is different from the split-tones that David Sanborn utilizes. David Sanborn was one of the first saxophonists to start playing on a mouthpiece with a substantial baffle, which helps speed up the airstream. The R&B growl doesn't require the ee and ay vowels needed to produce split-tones; rather, it requires a slower air stream and can be easily done using an older style mouthpiece (no baffle, large chamber). The technique also requires the saxophonist to produce a humming sound from the back of the throat so that a vibration is felt on the roof of the oral cavity/mouth area. The oh vowel shape best facilitates the R&B growl as it keeps the throat open so the air stream is wide and slow, as opposed to the faster/narrower ee and ay vowel shapes.

In order to explore this sensation, try humming your favorite simple melody. Do you feel the humming/vibration near the front of your mouth or nose? Can you focus the humming/vibration so that you feel it resonating in your throat and/or back portion of the roof of your mouth near your wisdom teeth/molars? If you can feel the humming in the back of your throat/back part of your mouth, and if you can make sure your throat is making the oh vowel shape, then the R&B growl will come easily for you.

FAST TEMPOS

How to Hold the Sax

Fast tempo performances require precision. Wasted energy and movement will keep you from properly executing fast passages. You must hold the saxophone in a way that feels comfortable and natural. The neck strap should be adjusted so that the saxophone is balanced and naturally hangs at a position where the mouthpiece meets your lips/embouchure without having to lift the saxophone via the thumb rest. Your hands have to be relaxed for fast passages; if your wrists and thumbs have tension, it will be difficult to execute these. Tension can also lead to tendonitis. Also, you don't want any wasted motion in the pinky and palm keys, making this natural position very important.

Finger Positions

Don't lift your fingers off the keys of the saxophone. It creates a great deal of wasted motion. It's a terrible habit, since it's impossible to play fast if you're consciously putting energy into lifting your fingers off the keys. Like the old saying "Work smarter, not harder," just let the springs of the saxophone do the work for you. If your fingers aren't nimble, you won't be able to play fast tempos.

I have often put double-sided tape on the pearls of students' saxophones so they can feel their fingers unnecessarily coming off the pearls and wrecking their technique. If in doubt, try taping your fingers to gauge your own technique and practice from there. Again, it's a good idea to look at your hand position in a mirror while practicing.

Alternate Fingerings

Here are some alternate fingerings that will improve your technique:

Alternate Fingerings

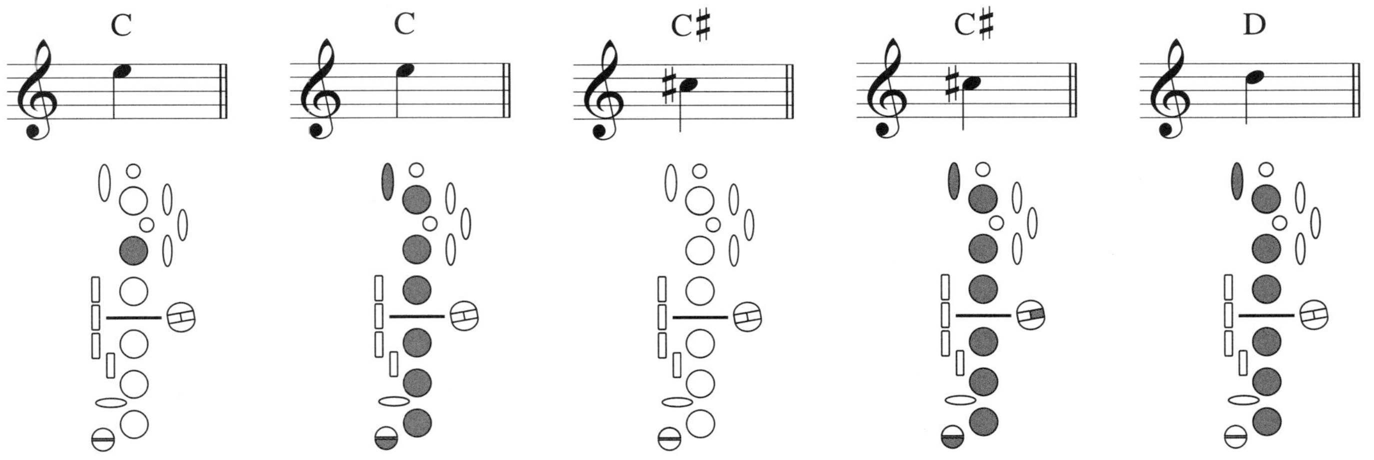

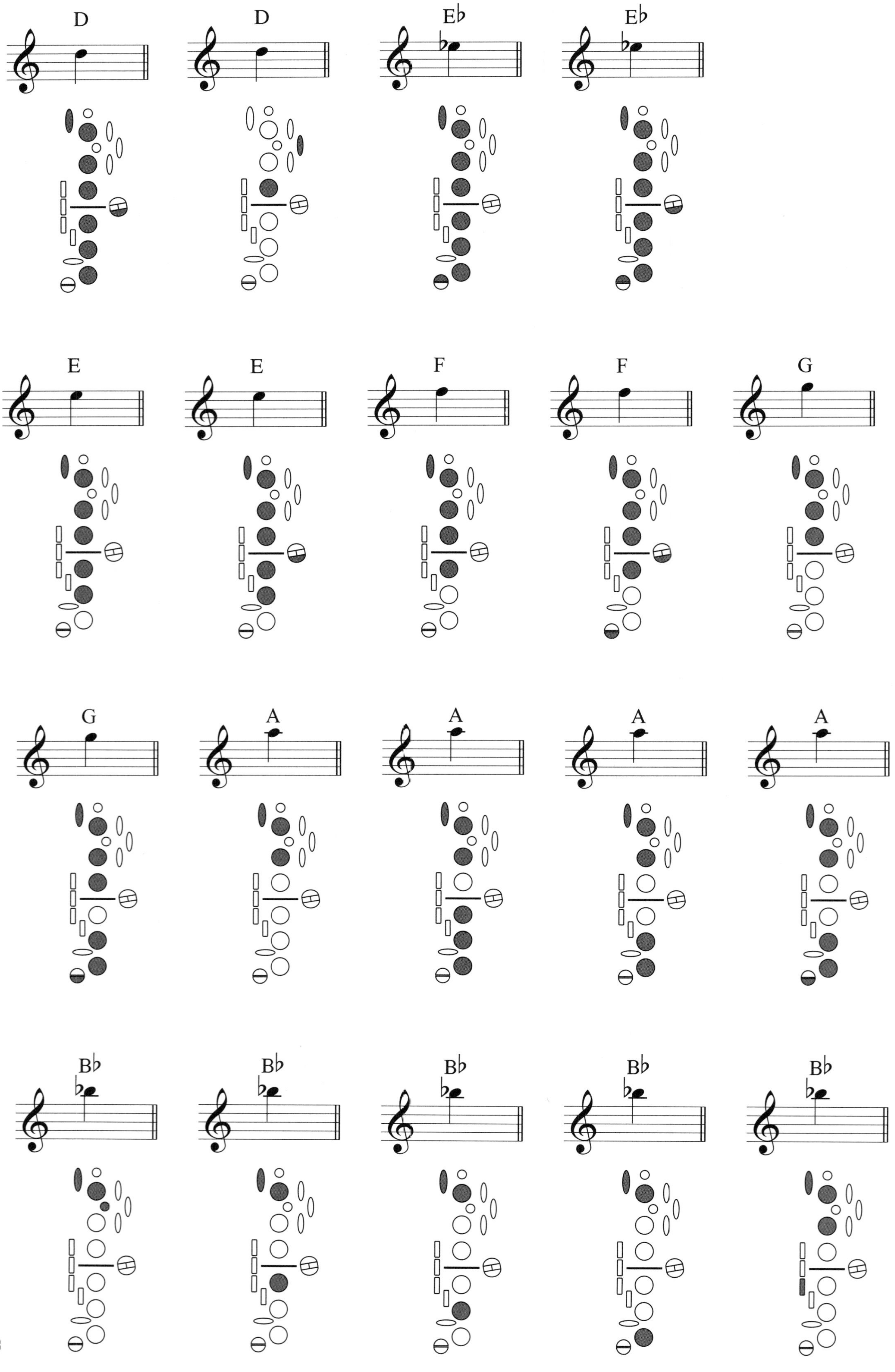
D
D
E♭
E♭
E
E
F
F
G
G
A
A
A
A
B♭
B♭
B♭
B♭
B♭

B♭

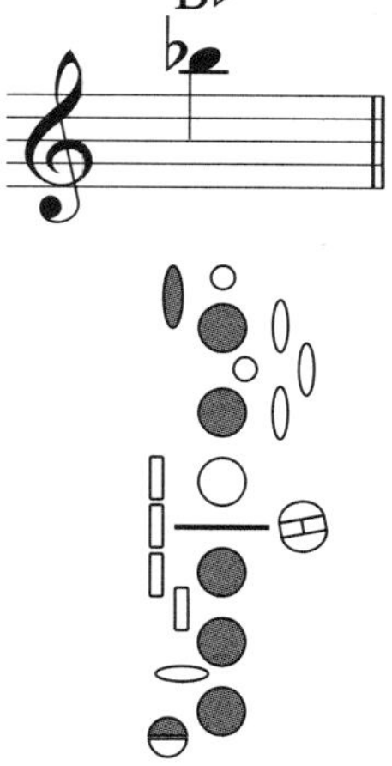

B♭

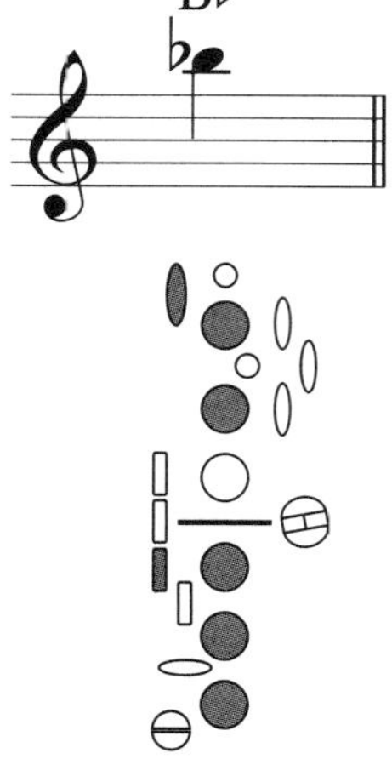

C

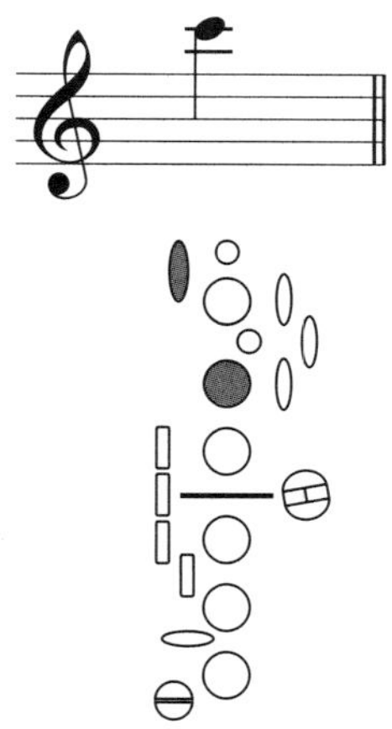

C

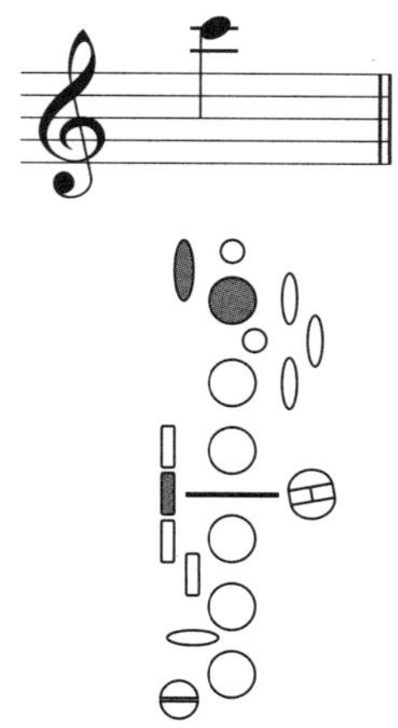

C

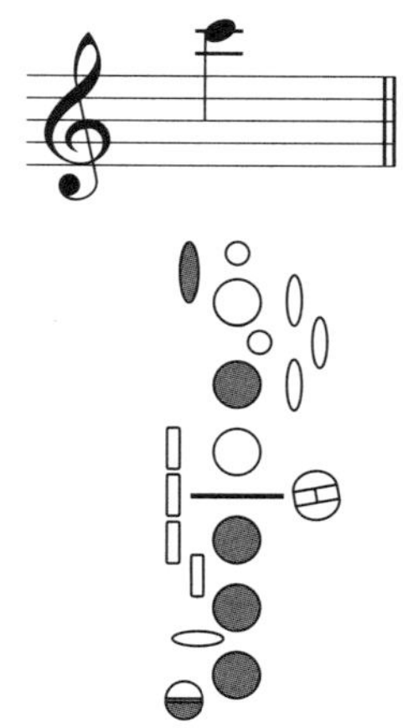

D

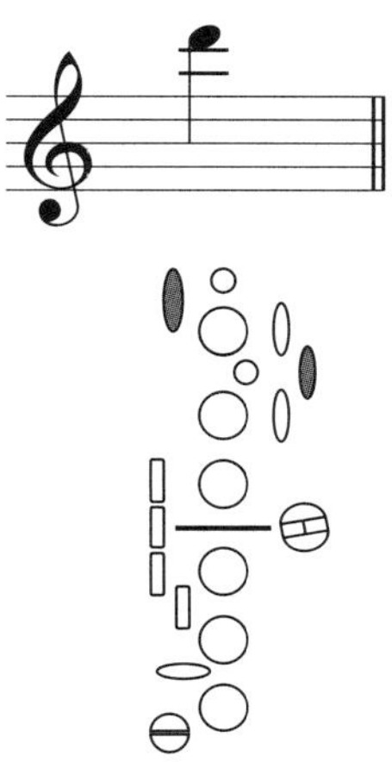

D

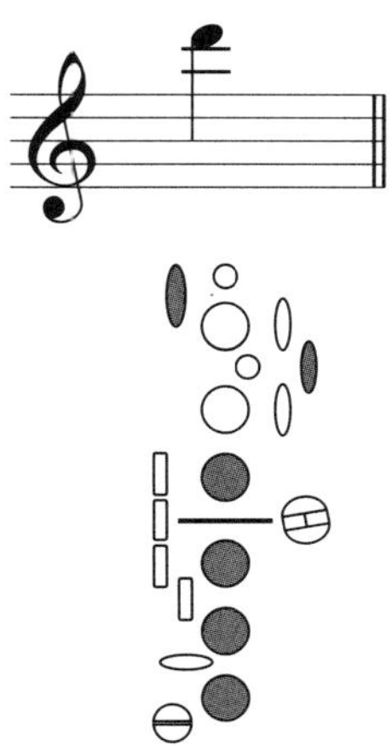

E

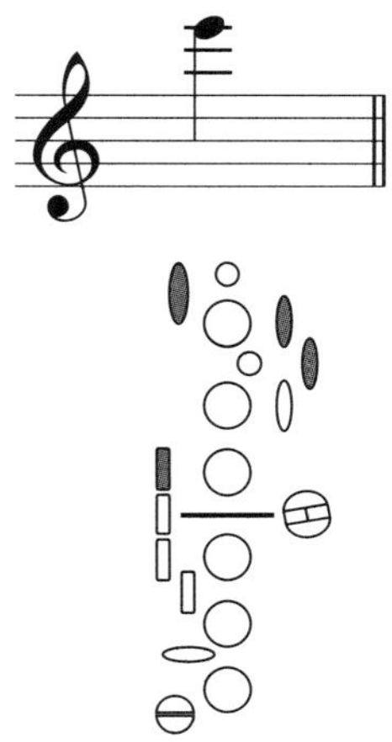

E

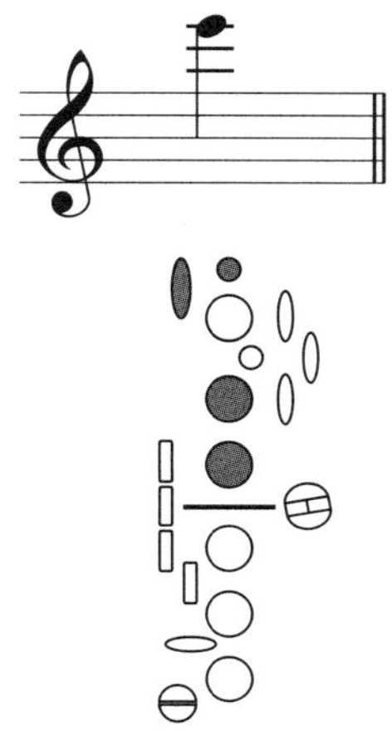

E

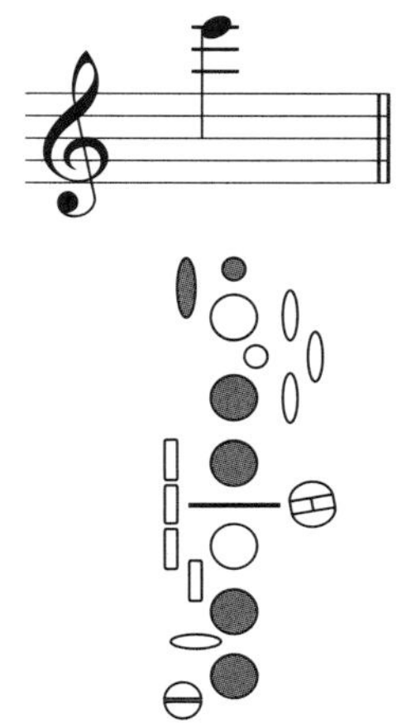

F

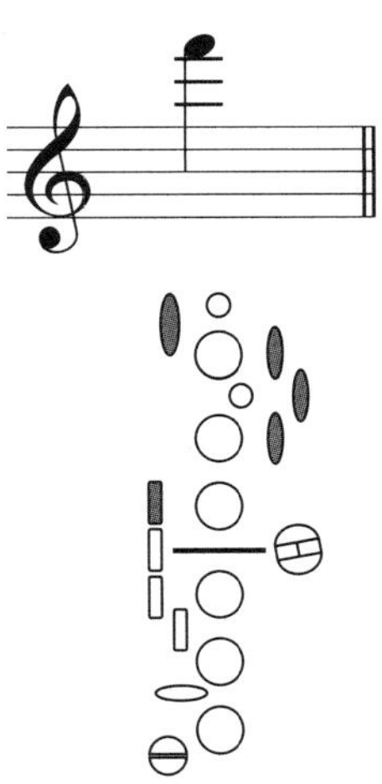

F

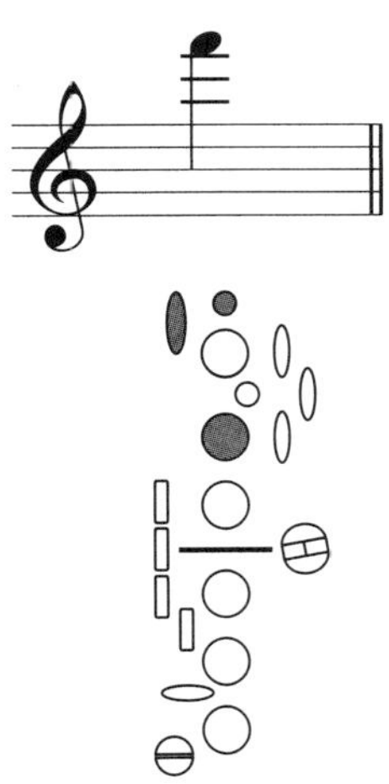

F

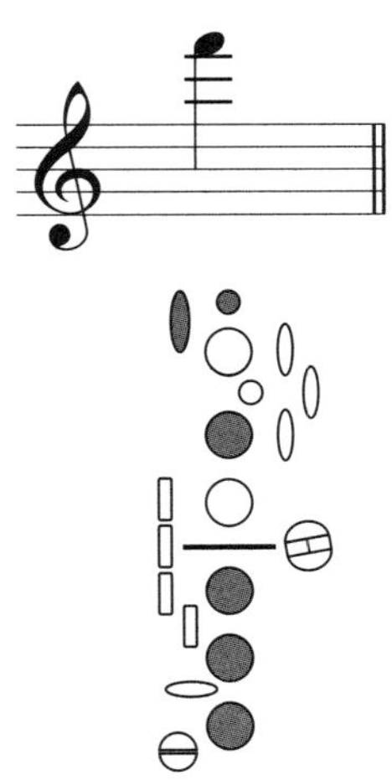

TO TONGUE OR NOT TO TONGUE

What is your definition of tonguing?

____

____

Many students think tonguing simply consists of using your tongue to stop the air/sound. While this is partially correct, there are many types and styles of tonguing. Too elementary an understanding of tonguing would be the equivalent of thinking that all you need to know to drive a car is that the gas pedal is on the right and the brake pedal is on the left.

Explanation of Different Tonguing Techniques

Define the following terms:

- Slurring: ______________________________
- Attack: ______________________________
- Cutoff: ______________________________
- Accent: ______________________________
- Articulation: ______________________________
- Phrase: ______________________________

These are a few of the concepts that go into understanding tonguing and cutoffs. Although not generally discussed as much, cutoffs are as important as tonguing for proper technique. The importance of knowing how to properly work the brakes on a car is equivalent to a saxophonist having good control of their cutoffs. When you tongue a note, know where your tongue is currently making contact. Is it the reed? Is it the tip of the mouthpiece? Most of the time, your tongue should be positioned so you can create a seal between the reed and the tip of the mouthpiece. If you hit only the tip of the reed with your tongue, you'll quickly wear out or chip the reed, not to mention possibly giving your tongue minor paper-cut-like abrasions. Don't stop your airflow while tonguing; that would be like turning your car engine off when you hit the brakes.

Here is a quick test. Once your mouthpiece, reed, and ligature are in place, put your mouth on the mouthpiece using normal playing embouchure. Then put your hand at the back of the mouthpiece so that it forms a seal. Next, put some air into the mouthpiece. Is air leaking from anywhere? Absolutely no air should be leaking and your embouchure should form a proper seal around the mouthpiece. Tonguing, cutoffs, tuning, etc. are difficult if you have a leaky embouchure, so do a quick spot check every few months. Also note that sometimes the table and rails on your mouthpiece can become uneven from use, which can make them less "reed friendly" and slightly leaky/problematic.

It's important to mention that, regardless of tonguing or slurring, the time values remain the same. For developing saxophonists, tonguing is often the kiss of death for proper time and groove. I have heard many educators make a push for completely slurring lines and phrases for this reason. Ultimately, you're the artist and it's your decision how you want to sound.

Here are some tonguing options to add to your toolbox so you can decide for yourself "to tongue or not to tongue":

- Da: Syllable for an articulated note. Begins with an attack but doesn't end with one.
- Ah: Syllable for a slurred note.
- Dot: Syllable that is accented. Begins with an attack and ends with a tongue cutoff.
- Slurring: Absence of tonguing.
- Cutoffs: Using the tongue to end a note. Notes are full value and the tongue makes the release of the note sound and feel accented.

Here are a few tips for where to tongue when no accents are indicated in the music by the composer, conductor, or arranger:

- When playing jazz passages with a swing feel, try slurring from the "offbeat" or "anticipated" eighth note to the eighth note that is on the beat.
- Try tonguing and/or accenting only the top notes of the phrase or melodic contour of each motif à la Charlie Parker and Cannonball Adderly.
- Try using very little tonguing while playing and ask yourself whether it sounds better or worse. I think modern players generally use much less tonguing. Consider John Coltrane's development. In the late 1950s, Coltrane tongues like crazy on "Blue Trane" and "Blowing Session." Five years later, he's tonguing much less and using his signature "sheets of sound" more frequently.

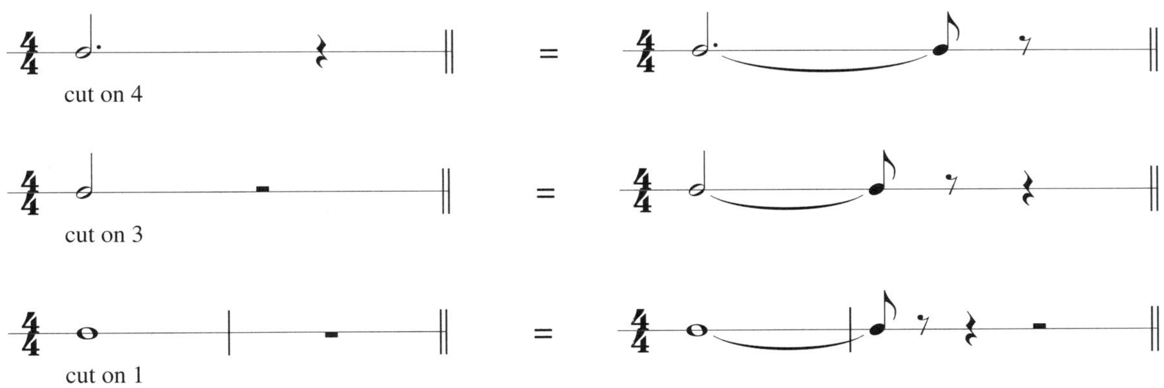

Experiment, because you'll have to decide what you prefer for your own musical statements and improvising. For awesome examples of players who use tonguing and accents to propel their lines, listen to Sonny Rollins and Johnny Griffin. While I caution everyone about over tonguing, Rollins and Griffin are two masters that all saxophone players should be familiar with.

Cross-Tonguing

Do you have any recordings of Von Freeman or Teddy Edwards?

Cross-tonguing is what I call a type of tonguing used by my mentor Von Freeman, along with Teddy Edwards and various saxophonists who tend to have "bluesy" inflections in their playing. It's not very complicated, but it takes some time and effort to master. Also note that overdoing it can be bad, so use cross-tonguing with caution.

Basically, your tongue is making contact with the reed and mouthpiece in an angled or crisscross fashion. It creates a broader attack with a lot of inflection, much like a blues guitarist slightly bends a string with the left hand while strumming with the right. Once mastered, it's fun to use in blues, rock, and old-achool jazz situations.

Snap Fingerings à la Cannonball

What I will call "snap fingerings" can commonly be heard in the playing of Cannonball Adderly and Charlie Parker, among others. It sounds almost like the players are articulating various points of a phrase without using their tongue. What they *are* doing is using a slight acceleration of their airstream, while making sure their finger movements are perfectly synchronized, so that certain notes "pop" and are more emphasized. This is different than being "accented" by being tongued; it has a slightly different sonic characteristic. Forget having the tongue involved, which might change the timing or spacing between notes. Instead, focus on using your fingers and airstream to make the notes "pop." Snap fingerings are a great technique for fast and/or double-time passages.

Slap Tongue: Classical, Getz

Once an extended technique, slap tonguing has become rather commonplace for the contemporary classical saxophonist. It produces a *percussive* sound. My favorite saxophonist to use slap tonguing in a very musical way is Stan Getz. Listen to a few Stan Getz recordings and you'll hear what I'm talking about. To create this effect, a vacuum is needed at the reed and mouthpiece to ensure a perfect seal. Generally, this is achieved by a slight intake of air with the tongue against the reed and then a quick burst of air as the tongue is removed from the reed. Slap tonguing is more pronounced when used in the lower notes of the saxophone. Give it a try!

MODERN HARMONY TIPS

Diminished

Diminished phrases are important to modern saxophonists of all genres. They are particularly fun to use over dominant chords when improvising. Here are some important scale exercises for ii–V7–I chord progressions that mathematically line up; they produce the 7th to 3rd resolution in many cases. These exercises are important for all saxophonists to master and incorporate into their practice. In this case, the diminished scale is played over the V7 chord and is configured using whole step–half step–whole step–half step–whole step–half step–whole step–half step intervals to produce the 7th to 3rd resolution.

Pattern 1

Pattern 2

Pattern 3

Locrian #2

The Locrian #2 starts off the first exercise. It begins on the 2nd and/or 9th scale degree. I have added a passing tone so that the "math" works nicely.

Must-Know Chord Progressions

Review these common chord progressions that saxophonists should be able to play at the piano. They will help you *hear*, *see*, and *feel* how chords resolve, which will ultimately enhance your playing. Piano voicings for 12-bar blues and 32-bar rhythm changes are shown below. Also, 12-bar blues and 32-bar rhythm changes are featured on the online video in the "You're in the Band" section. Feel free to play along! Both blues and rhythm changes are chock full of ii–V7–I and iii–VI7–ii–V7–I progressions.

12-Bar Blues

Rhythym Changes

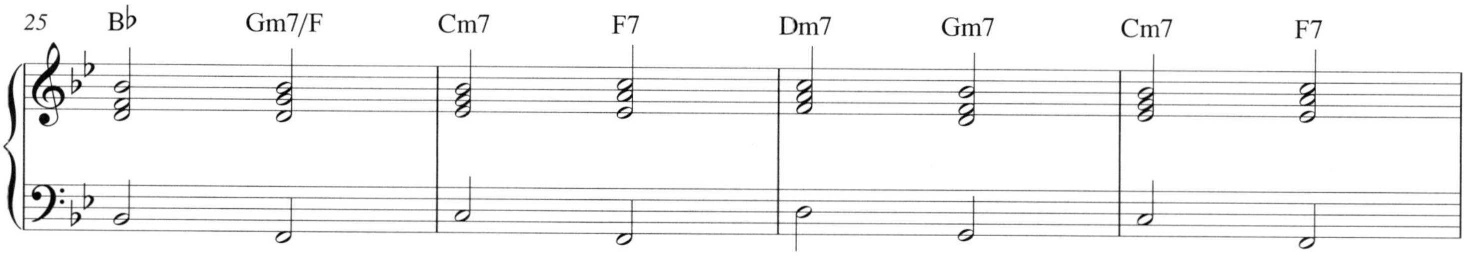
25
B♭
Gm7/F
Cm7
F7
Dm7
Gm7
Cm7
F7

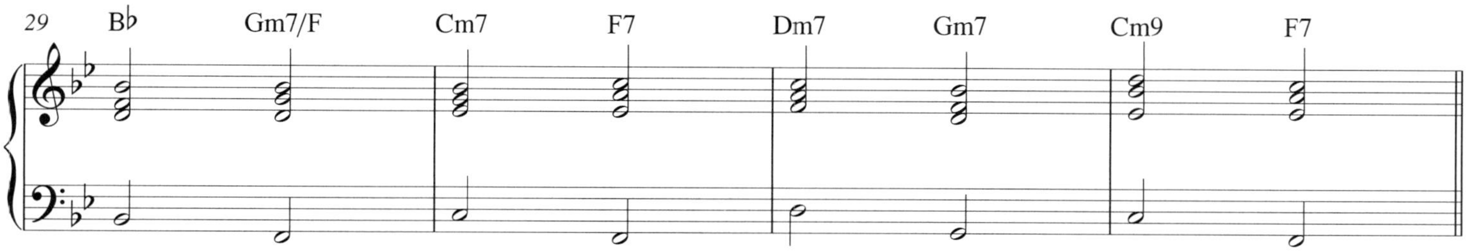
29
B♭
Gm7/F
Cm7
F7
Dm7
Gm7
Cm9
F7

COOL DOWN

Have You Had Any Hand Injuries?

I hope you have had no hand injuries! When I was 17 years old, my right middle finger was completely cut off and reattached. When I was 33, my left wrist was permanently damaged by a drunk driver who ignored a red light and plowed into my car. I have suffered torn ligaments and cartilage, which hasn't been fun. Fortunately, I've always had solid hand positioning and technique, which is the best defense for overcoming a traumatic injury, as well as preventing any repetitive stress injuries.

Hand Injuries

Simple Stretches So You Are Always "Good to Go"

Some people think they're helping by stretching, but over-stretching can result in micro tears of your muscles, ligaments, or tendons. Simple stretches are best; don't overdo it, because that can cause injuries. What works best for me? These great, simple stretches will keep your forearms flexible so tendinitis and other issues will be kept at bay. I practice the following two gentle exercises every day to get my muscles, wrists, and elbow joints moving and limber. Repeat each exercise about a dozen times.

1. Extend your arms in front of you, palms facing the down, and rotate your wrists back and forth like the motion of turning a door knob.
2. Slowly bend your wrist up toward you, and then go down in the opposite direction until the arms and wrists form a 90-degree angle.

How Not to Develop Repetitive Stress Injuries (and Drop Out of College)

My college roommate developed a bad case of tendinitis from practicing 12 hours a day and ultimately dropped out of college. I saw many specialists after my car accident and the best advice I received was "Let pain and swelling be your guide." It's up to you to take care of your most important instrument: your own body. If you feel tendinitis developing or any pain, take a break from practicing. Evaluate your body, posture, and hand positioning. Make sure you're not using your muscles to lift your fingers off the keys, because that's unnecessary; it's just wasted energy/movement that the body wasn't designed to endure. Remember that your strength and ability for closing your hands and fingers is far greater than the strength and ability to open them.

Remember to Work Smarter, Not Necessarily Harder (and Avoid Injuries)

Do you have a practice routine? I think solid, concentrated practice is far more beneficial than countless hours of random practicing. Quality, focused practice will also keep repetitive-stress injuries at bay. Here are a few sample practice routines that are about an hour long and will ensure solid results. It's better to work smarter than harder. Remember the value of quality over quantity!

Practice Schedule

When planning your practice schedule, it's important to be organized. Vary what you practice, just like an athlete changes up his daily workouts. An athlete wouldn't do seven straight days of bicep exercises, while ignoring other muscle groups, or practice the same exercises every single day. Similarly, you should alternate exercises and aim for a well-rounded routine. The following is an example of a seven-day practice schedule, but it's essential that you develop what works best for *you*. Only you know your strengths and weaknesses, so be honest and keep up the good work.

Day 1

- 20 minutes of long tones
- 20 minutes of technical facility
- 20 minutes of playing along with recordings

Day 2

- 10 minutes of long-tones
- 20 minutes of transcribing
- 30 minutes of composing

Day 3

- Same as Day 1

Day 4

- 10 minutes of long tones
- 20 minutes of piano scales and comping
- 30 minutes of memorizing one of your favorite standards

Day 5

- Same as day Day 1

Day 6

- 10 minutes of long tones
- 10 minutes of articulation
- 20 minutes of scales on your non-primary saxophone (i.e., if alto is your main sax, do these exercises on soprano, tenor, or bari)
- 20 minutes of working with a tuner. Make sure your embouchure is solid and that you're not pinching or puffing. It's beneficial to do this in front of a mirror. Practicing scales in whole notes and intervals in whole notes works great.

Day 7

- 20 minutes of memorizing a song or etude
- 20 minutes of composing bass lines for a chord progression or song
- 20 minutes of working on altissimo notes

SING TO ME!

Ask yourself the following questions:

- How often do I sing?
- Can I sing, hum, or whistle all the melodies I play on the saxophone?
- Can I sing a half-step interval *in tune*?
- Can I sing a minor 3rd interval *in tune*?

"If you can sing something, you can play it." James Moody told me that while I was in Charles Earland's band. At the time, I thought I could sing well and had fun scat singing backstage. Then I started *really* trying to match my voice to a tuner and with a piano, only to discover that my pitch needed work.

Intervals

Here are some practice ideas to explore that will help your *internal* sense of pitch. Eventually, you'll have a better *external* sense of pitch, which will enhance your ability to sit in with bands who you haven't played with before. You will soon *hear* the key, chords, and melodies without the need for sheet music or a discussion about the tunes. That's a valuable skill!

It's important to visualize the keyboard while singing intervals because this will help develop your ear. I think it's best to visualize the keyboard as being symmetrical – from A up and G down. Look at the diagram below. A up to E makes a perfect 5th interval and G down to C makes a perfect 5th interval; they look like a mirror image of each other. Interestingly, on the saxophone, octave key G to A is where the octave breaks. The venting of the octave pip on the body tube, while G and/or G♯ are played, switches to the octave vent on the neck of the saxophone when A is played. The octave break is often a trouble spot, so a lot of the exercises in this book will help you overcome this issue.

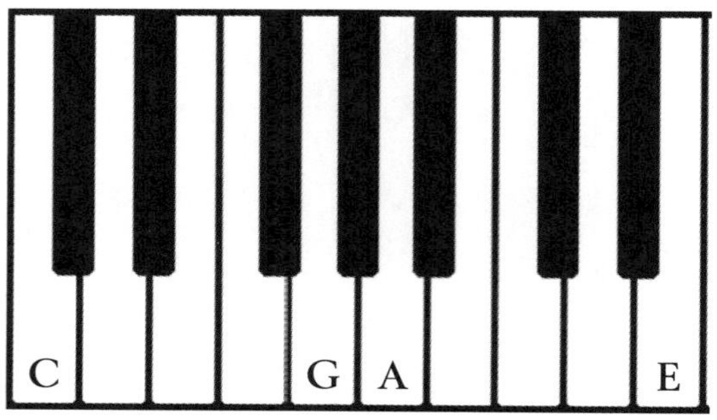

Using the keyboard diagram, write in the names of all the notes and as many intervals as you can from A ascending and G descending.

Intervals are important for building up your technique as a saxophonist. That is why I have included some saxophone exercises at the back of this book dealing with perfect 4th intervals, pentatonic scales, saxophone lines based off of piano chords and shapes, 9th intervals, enclosures where you use half steps and whole steps to emphasize a desired note, exercises based off of modes, and more.

Melodies

Now that you've had fun with intervals and ear training, use a few of those intervals to write some melodies. Write a melody to play along with me for the Modal Study track on the online video.

Modal Study

B-flat Instruments

Fm7
Em7

E-flat Instruments

- Hint: Some people use *solfège* to internalize pitches, while others sing the pitch by letter name or simply sing "do" or "oo" vowel sounds. Try all of them and stick with the one that feels most natural and comfortable for *you*. Also, be sure to associate pitches with the beginning of songs. For example, the first melody note of "Bye Bye Blackbird" in F concert pitch, which is the key it is most commonly played in, is A concert.

Here are some 12-tone rows. Arnold Schoenberg, Anton Webern, and other composers made them commonplace in Classical music written after World War II. Can you write a 12-tone melody (without repeating the pitch in those 12 notes)?

In modern music, a tetrachord is any four-note segment of a scale or tone row, not necessarily related to a particular system of turning. Traditionally in music theory, a tetrachord is a series of four tones filling in the interval of a perfect 4th. (Coltrane was fond of tetrachords.) A V–I–IV progression often is based on tetrachords. Scales built on chromatic tetrachords continue to be used in the music of the Middle East and India. Milton Babbitt's serial theory extends the term tetrachord to mean a four-note segment of a 12-tone row.

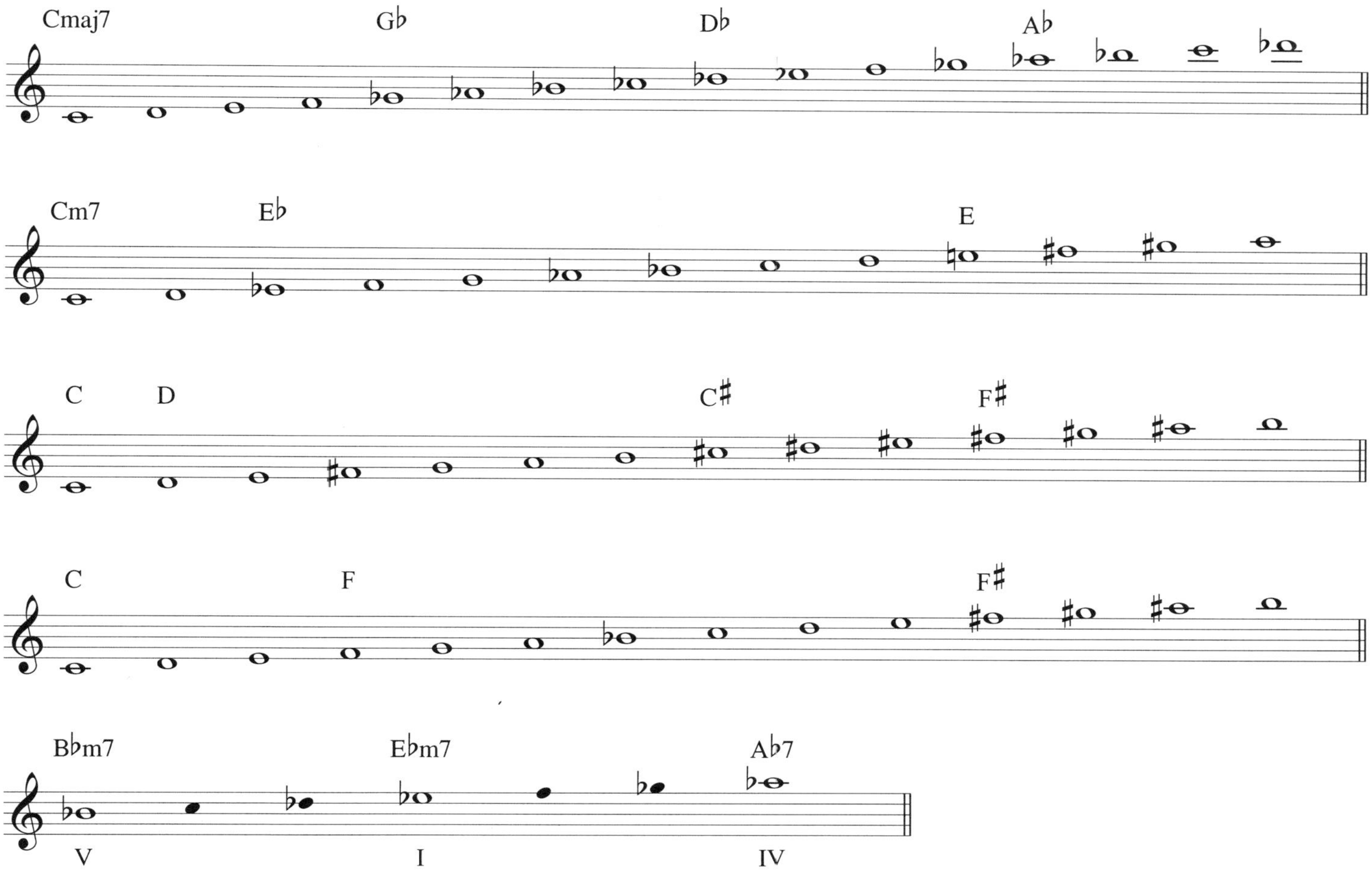

Here is a polyphonic complex of three different tetrachords:

Bass Lines

Here are some bass lines written in treble clef for the saxophone. Can you play through them and write some of your own? Can you do them in all 12 keys?

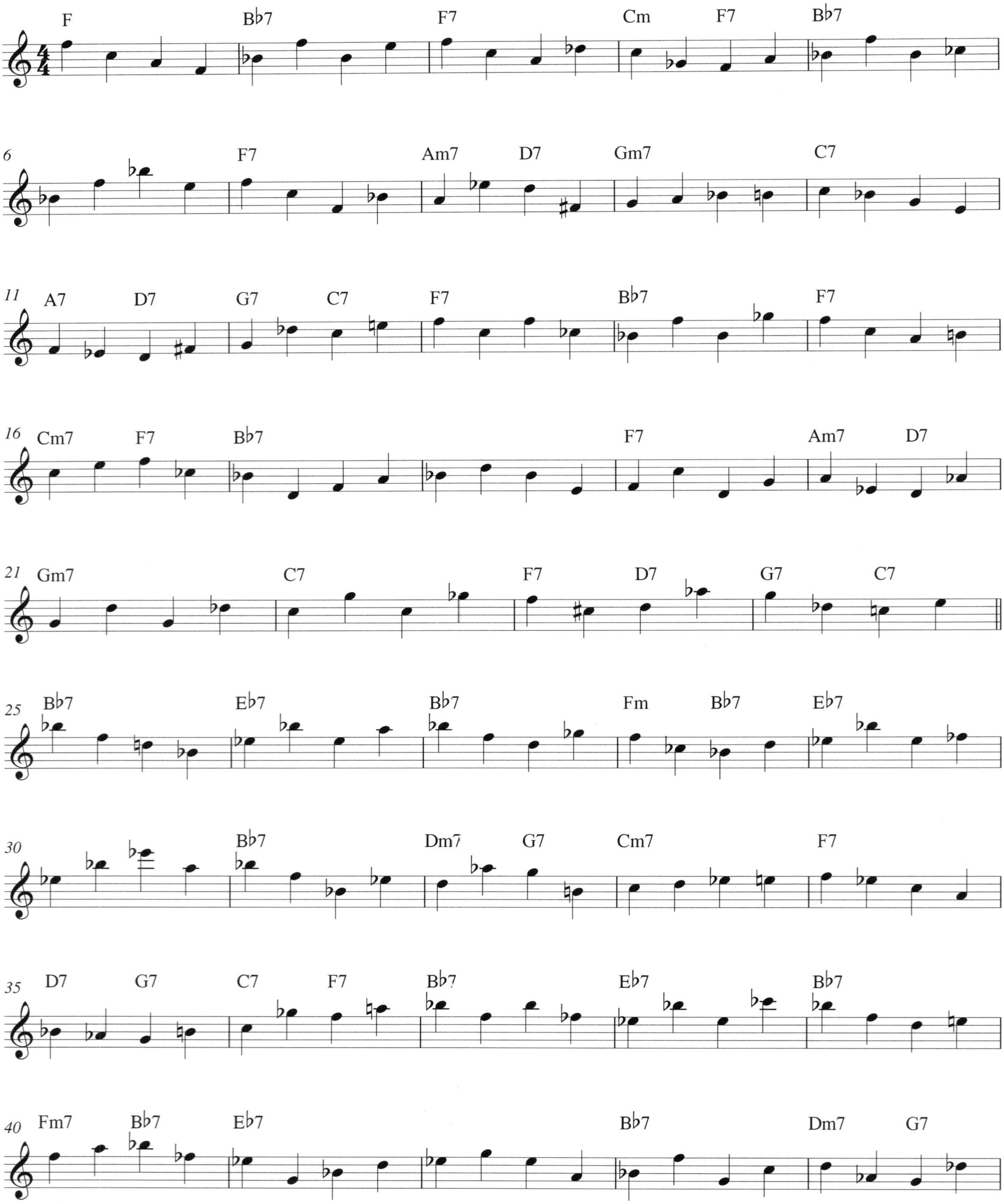

45 Cm7 F7 B♭7 G7 C7 F7
49 E♭7 A♭7 E♭7 B♭m E♭7 A♭7
54 E♭7 Gm7 C7 Fm7 B♭7
59 G7 C7 F7 B♭7 E♭7 A♭7 E♭7
64 B♭m7 E♭7 A♭7 E♭7 Gm7 C7
69 Fm7 B♭7 E♭7 C7 F7 B♭7
73 A♭7 D♭7 A♭7 E♭m A♭7 D♭7
78 A♭7 Cm7 F7 B♭m7 E♭7
83 C7 F7 B♭7 E♭7 A♭7 D♭7 A♭7

88 E♭m7 A♭7 D♭7 A♭7 Cm7 F7
93 B♭m7 E♭7 A♭7 F7 B♭7 E♭7
97 D♭7 G♭7 D♭7 A♭m D♭7 G♭7
102 D♭7 Fm7 B♭7 E♭m7 A♭7
107 F7 B♭7 E♭7 A♭7 D♭7 G♭7 D♭7
112 A♭m7 D♭7 G♭7 D♭7 Fm7 B♭7
117 E♭m7 A♭7 D♭7 B♭7 E♭7 A♭7
121 G♭7 B7 G♭7 D♭m G♭7 B7
126 G♭7 B♭m7 E♭7 A♭m7 D♭7

131 B♭7 E♭7 A♭7 D♭7 G♭7 B7 G♭7
136 D♭m7 G♭7 B7 G♭7 B♭m7 E♭7
141 A♭m7 D♭7 G♭7 E♭7 A♭7 D♭7
145 B7 E7 B7 F♯m7 B7 E7
150 B7 E♭m7 A♭7 D♭m7 F♯7
155 E♭7 A♭7 D♭7 F♯7 B7 E7 B7
160 F♯m7 B7 E7 B7 E♭m7 A♭7
165 D♭m7 F♯7 B7 A♭7 D♭7 F♯7
169 E7 A7 E7 Bm7 E7 A7

174 E7 Abm7 Db7 F#m7 B7
179 Ab7 Db7 F#7 B7 E7 A7 E7
184 Bm7 E7 A7 E7 Abm7 Db7
189 F#m7 B7 E7 Db7 F#7 B7
193 A7 D7 A7 Em7 A7
197 D7 A7 Dbm7 F#7
201 Bm7 E7 Db7 F#7 B7 E7
205 A7 D7 A7 Em7 A7
209 D7 A7 Dbm7 F#7

213 Bm7 E7 A7 F♯7 B7 E7
217 D7 G7 D7 Am7 D7
221 G7 D7 F♯m7 B7
225 Em7 A7 F♯7 B7 E7 A7
229 D7 G7 D7 Am7 D7
233 G7 D7 F♯m7 B7
237 Em7 A7 D7 B7 E7 A7
241 G7 C7 G7 Dm7 G7
245 C7 G7 Bm7 E7

249 Am7 D7 B7 E7 A7 D7
253 G7 C7 G7 Dm7 G7
257 C7 G7 Bm7 E7
261 Am7 D7 G7 E7 A7
265 C7 F7 C7 Gm7 C7 F7
270 C7 Em7 A7 Dm7 G7
275 E7 A7 D7 G7 C7 F7 C7
280 Gm7 C7 F7 C7 Em7 A7
285 Dm7 G7 C7 A7 D7

ETUDES FOR FURTHER STUDY

Practice these exercises, beginning with the metronome set to ♩ = 60. Increase the tempo gradually as the passages become more comfortable and more controlled.

Enclosures

Diminished Enclosures

4ths

Now we start in Dorian mode, depart from it using the stabilizing nature of quartal harmony to leave the mode and obscure tonic or potentially even move it altogether.

Now we start in Dorian mode, depart from it using the stabilizing nature of quartal harmony to leave the mode and obscure tonic or potentially even move it altogether.

9ths

11ths

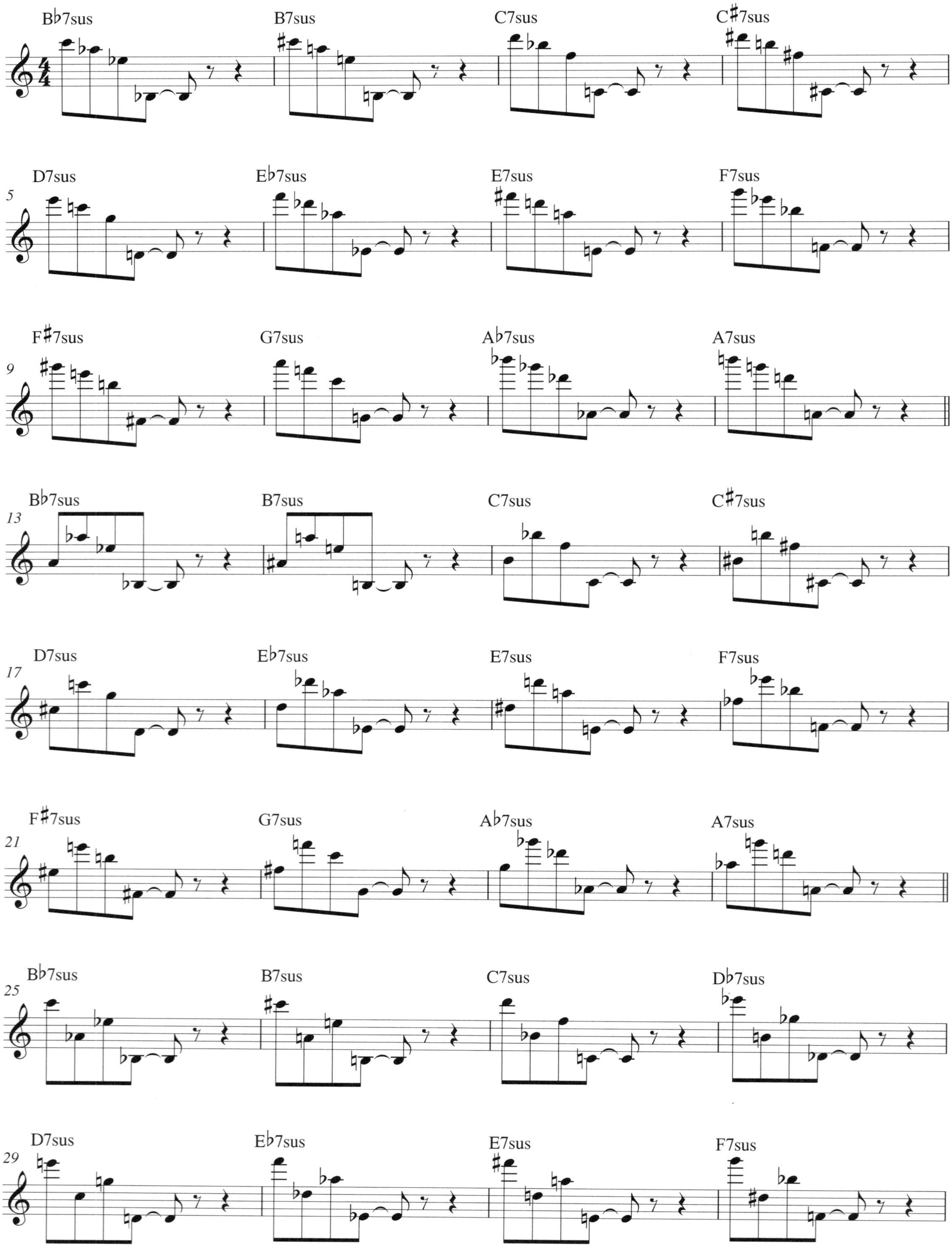
Bb7sus
B7sus
C7sus
C#7sus
5
D7sus
Eb7sus
E7sus
F7sus
9
F#7sus
G7sus
Ab7sus
A7sus
13
Bb7sus
B7sus
C7sus
C#7sus
17
D7sus
Eb7sus
E7sus
F7sus
21
F#7sus
G7sus
Ab7sus
A7sus
25
Bb7sus
B7sus
C7sus
Db7sus
29
D7sus
Eb7sus
E7sus
F7sus

33
F♯7sus
G7sus
A♭7sus
A7sus
37
B♭7sus
B7sus
C7sus
C♯7sus
41
D7sus
E♭7sus
E7sus
F7sus
45
F♯7sus
G7sus
A♭7sus
A7sus
49
B♭13
B13
C13
C♯13
53
D13
E♭13
E13
F13
57
F♯13
G13
A♭13
A13
61
B♭13
B13
C13
C♯13

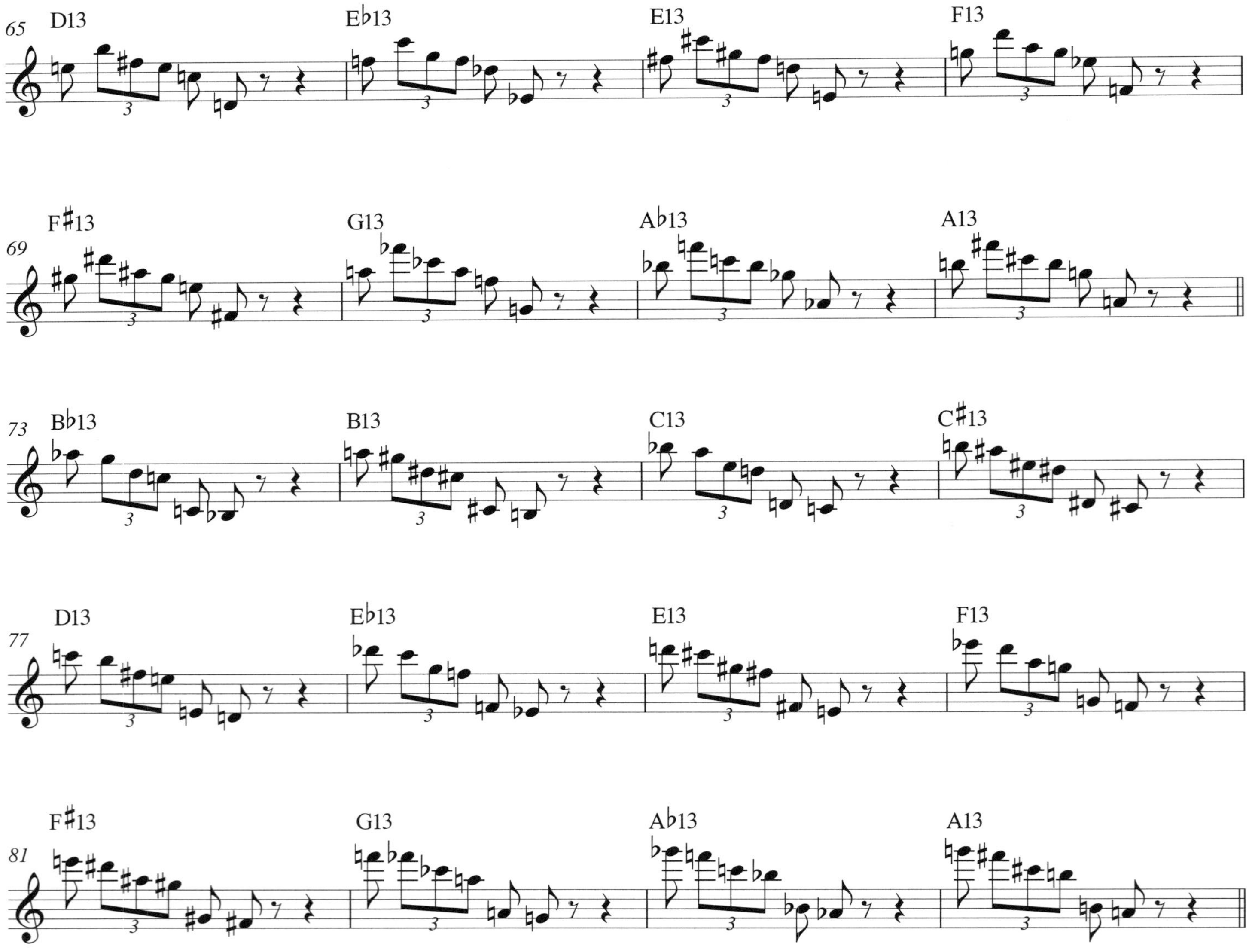

Cut-time Study #1

double time
11 Am7♭5
D7♭9
Gm7
13 Dm7♭5
G7♭9
Cm7
double time
17 Dm7♭5
G7♭9
Cm7
19 Gm7♭5
C7♭9
Fm7
double time
23 Gm7♭5
C7♭9
Fm7
25 Cm7♭5
F7♭9
B♭m7
double time
29 Cm7♭5
F7♭9
B♭m7
31 Fm7♭5
B♭7♭9
E♭m7
double time
35 Fm7♭5
B♭7♭9
E♭m7

37 Bbm7b5
Eb7b9
Abm7
double time
41 Bbm7b5
Eb7b9
Abm7
43 Ebm7b5
Ab7b9
Dbm7
double time
47 Ebm7b5
Ab7b9
Dbm7
49 Abm7b5
Db7b9
Gbm7
double time
53 Abm7b5
Db7b9
Gbm7
55 Dbm7b5
Gb7b9
Bm7
double time
59 Dbm7b5
Gb7b9
Bm7
61 Gbm7b5
B7b9
Em7

Cut-time Study #2

19
23
25
29
double time
31
35
double time
37
41
double time
43

double time
47
49
double time
53
55
double time
59
61
double time
65
67
double time
71

Modes

C Ionian
ascending 3rds
5
descending 3rds
9
ascending 4ths
13
descending 4ths
17
ascending 5ths
21
descending 5ths
25
ascending 6ths
29
descending 6ths
33
ascending 7ths

37
descending 7ths
41
ascending to descending 3rds
45
descending to ascending 3rds
49
ascending to descending 4ths
53
descending to ascending 4ths
57
ascending to descending 5ths
61
descending to ascending 5ths
65
ascending to descending 6ths
69
descending to ascending 6ths

73
ascending to descending 7ths
77
descending to ascending 7ths
81
C Dorian
85
ascending 3rds
89
descending 3rds
93
ascending 4ths
97
descending 4ths
101
ascending 5ths
105
descending 5ths

109 ascending 6ths
113 descending 6ths
117 ascending 7ths
121 descending 7ths
125 ascending to descending 3rds
129 descending to ascending 3rds
133 ascending to descending 4ths
137 descending to ascending 4ths
141 ascending to descending 5ths

145
descending to ascending 5ths
149
ascending to descending 6ths
153
descending to ascending 6ths
157
ascending to descending 7ths
161
descending to ascending 7ths
165
C Phrygian
ascending 3rds
169
descending 3rds
173
ascending 4ths
177
descending 4ths

181
ascending 5ths
185
descending 5ths
189
ascending 6ths
193
descending 6ths
197
ascending 7ths
201
descending 7ths
205
ascending to descending 3rds
209
descending to ascending 3rds
213
ascending to descending 4ths

217
descending to ascending 4ths
221
ascending to descending 5ths
225
descending to ascending 5ths
229
ascending to descending 6ths
233
descending to ascending 6ths
237
ascending to descending 7ths
241
descending to ascending 7ths
245
C Lydian
249
ascending 3rds

253
descending 3rds
257
ascending 4ths
261
descending 4ths
265
ascending 5ths
269
descending 5ths
273
ascending 6ths
277
descending 6ths
281
ascending 7ths
285
descending 7ths

289 ascending to descending 3rds

293 descending to ascending 3rds

297 ascending to descending 4ths

301 descending to ascending 4ths

305 ascending to descending 5ths

309 descending to ascending 5ths

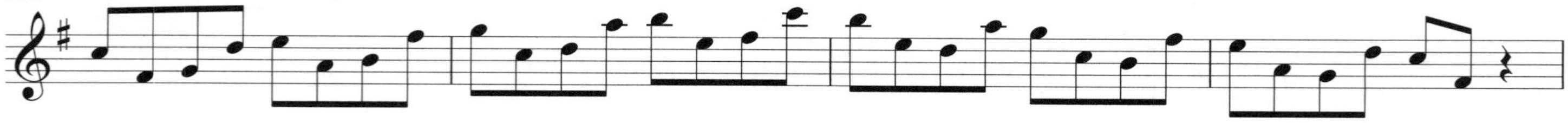

313 ascending to descending 6ths

317 descending to ascending 6ths

321 ascending to descending 7ths

325
descending to ascending 7ths
329
C Mixolydian
ascending 3rds
333
descending 3rds
337
ascending 4ths
341
descending 4ths
345
ascending 5ths
349
descending 5ths
353
ascending 6ths
357
descending 6ths

361
ascending 7ths
365
descending 7ths
369
ascending to descending 3rds
373
descending to ascending 3rds
377
ascending to descending 4ths
381
descending to ascending 4ths
385
ascending to descending 5ths
389
descending to ascending 5ths
393
ascending to descending 6ths

397
descending to ascending 6ths
401
ascending to descending 7ths
405
descending to ascending 7ths
409
C Aeolian
413
ascending 3rds
417
descending 3rds
421
ascending 4ths
425
descending 4ths
429
ascending 5ths

433
descending 5ths
437
ascending 6ths
441
descending 6ths
445
ascending 7ths
449
descending 7ths
453
ascending to descending 3rds
457
descending to ascending 3rds
461
ascending to descending 4ths
465
descending to ascending 4ths

469
ascending to descending 5ths
473
descending to ascending 5ths
477
ascending to descending 6ths
481
descending to ascending 6ths
485
ascending to descending 7ths
489
descending to ascending 7ths
493
C Locrian
ascending 3rds
497
descending 3rds
501
ascending 4ths

505
descending 4ths
509
ascending 5ths
513
descending 5ths
517
ascending 6ths
521
descending 6ths
525
ascending 7ths
529
descending 7ths
533
ascending to descending 3rds
537
descending to ascending 3rds

541
ascending to descending 4ths
545
descending to ascending 4ths
549
ascending to descending 5ths
553
descending to ascending 5ths
557
ascending to descending 6ths
561
descending to ascending 6ths
565
ascending to descending 7ths
569
descending to ascending 7ths
573

Pentatonic Study

Melodic Minor Study

37
descending 7ths
41
ascending to descending 3rds
45
descending to ascending 3rds
49
ascending to descending 4ths
53
descending to ascending 4ths
57
ascending to descending 5ths
61
descending to ascending 5ths
65
ascending to descending 6ths
69
descending to ascending 6ths

73
ascending to descending 7ths
77
descending to ascending 7ths
81
A
2nd mode of melodic minor
85
ascending 3rds
89
descending 3rds
93
ascending 4ths
97
descending 4ths
101
ascending 5ths
105
descending 5ths

109 ascending 6ths
113 descending 6ths
117 ascending 7ths
121 descending 7ths
125 ascending to descending 3rds
129 descending to ascending 3rds
133 ascending to descending 4ths
137 descending to ascending 4ths
141 ascending to descending 5ths

145
descending to ascending 5ths
149
ascending to descending 6ths
153
descending to ascending 6ths
157
ascending to descending 7ths
161
descending to ascending 7ths
A
165
3rd mode of melodic minor
ascending 3rds
169
descending 3rds
173
ascending 4ths
177
descending 4ths

181
ascending 5ths
185
descending 5ths
189
ascending 6ths
193
descending 6ths
197
ascending 7ths
201
descending 7ths
205
ascending to descending 3rds
209
descending to ascending 3rds
213
ascending to descending 4ths

217
descending to ascending 4ths
221
ascending to descending 5ths
225
descending to ascending 5ths
229
ascending to descending 6ths
233
descending to ascending 6ths
237
ascending to descending 7ths
241
descending to ascending 7ths
245
A
4th mode of melodic minor (Lydian dominant)
249
ascending 3rds

253 descending 3rds
257 ascending 4ths
261 descending 4ths
265 ascending 5ths
269 descending 5ths
273 ascending 6ths
277 descending 6ths
281 ascending 7ths
285 descending 7ths

289 ascending to descending 3rds
293 descending to ascending 3rds
297 ascending to descending 4ths
301 descending to ascending 4ths
305 ascending to descending 5ths
309 descending to ascending 5ths
313 ascending to descending 6ths
317 descending to ascending 6ths
321 ascending to descending 7ths

325
descending to ascending 7ths
A
329
5th mode of melodic minor
ascending 3rds
333
descending 3rds
337
ascending 4ths
341
descending 4ths
345
ascending 5ths
349
descending 5ths
353
ascending 6ths
357
descending 6ths

361
ascending 7ths
365
descending 7ths
369
ascending to descending 3rds
373
descending to ascending 3rds
377
ascending to descending 4ths
381
descending to ascending 4ths
385
ascending to descending 5ths
389
descending to ascending 5ths
393
ascending to descending 6ths

397
descending to ascending 6ths
401
ascending to descending 7ths
405
descending to ascending 7ths
409
A
6th mode of melodic minor
413
ascending 3rds
417
descending 3rds
421
ascending 4ths
425
descending 4ths
429
ascending 5ths

433 descending 5ths
437 ascending 6ths
441 descending 6ths
445 ascending 7ths
449 descending 7ths
453 ascending to descending 3rds
457 descending to ascending 3rds
461 ascending to descending 4ths
465 descending to ascending 4ths

469 ascending to descending 5ths
473 descending to ascending 5ths
477 ascending to descending 6ths
481 descending to ascending 6ths
485 ascending to descending 7ths
489 descending to ascending 7ths
A
493 7th mode of melodic minor
ascending 3rds
497
descending 3rds
501
ascending 4ths

505
descending 4ths
509
ascending 5ths
513
descending 5ths
517
ascending 6ths
521
descending 6ths
525
ascending 7ths
529
descending 7ths
533
ascending to descending 3rds
537
descending to ascending 3rds

541
ascending to descending 4ths
545
descending to ascending 4ths
549
ascending to descending 5ths
553
descending to ascending 5ths
557
ascending to descending 6ths
561
descending to ascending 6ths
565
ascending to descending 7ths
569
descending to ascending 7ths
573

Mighty Burner

By Frank Catalano

28
8va
31
(8va)
34
(8va)
37
(8va)
40
(8va)
3
3
43
3
46
3
49
51
53
3

Trane System

Modes Generated by the Major Scale

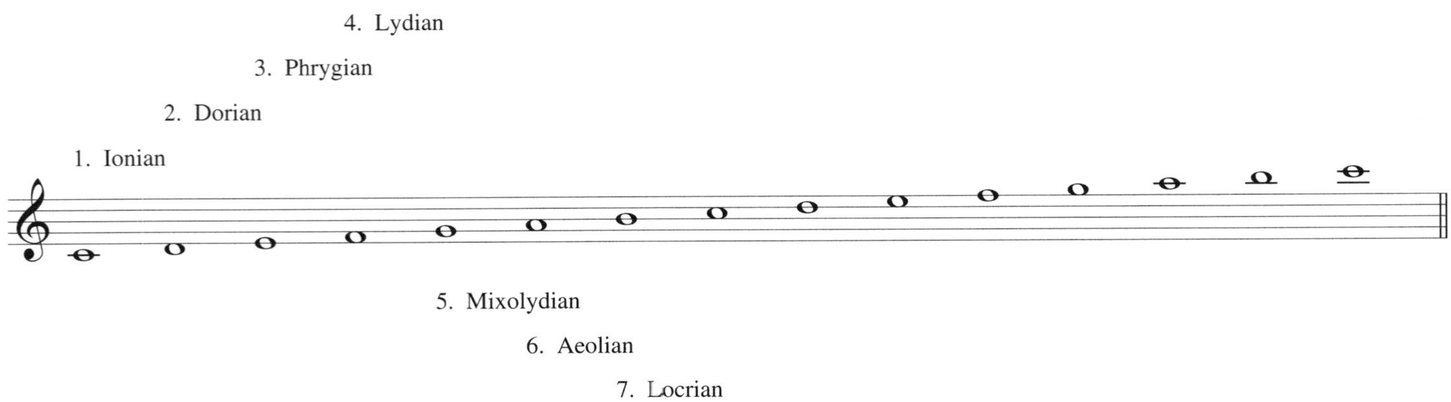

Modes Generated by the Harmonic Minor Scale

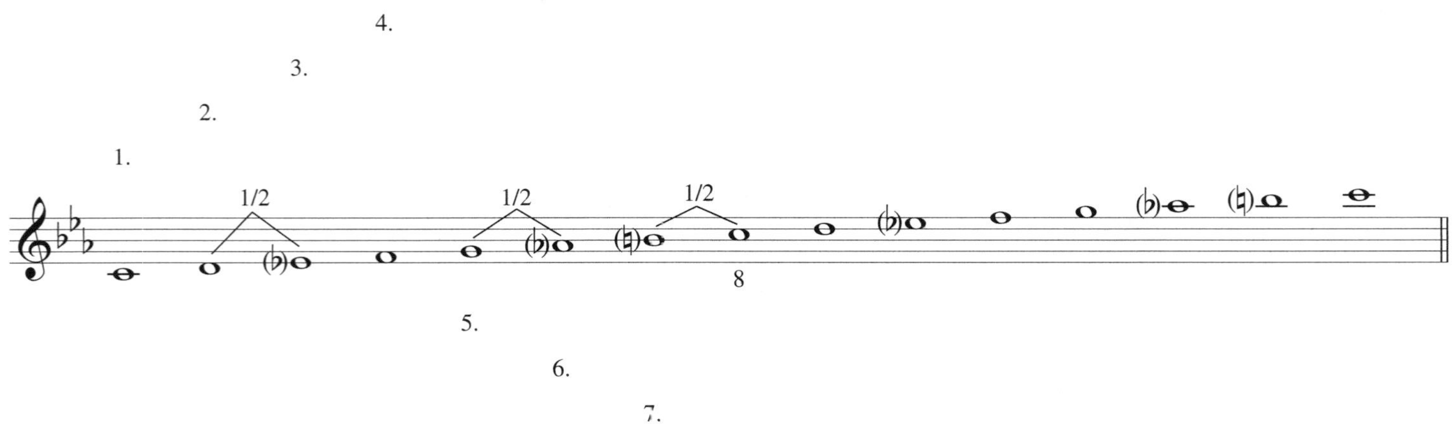

Modes Generated by the ascending Melodic Minor Scale

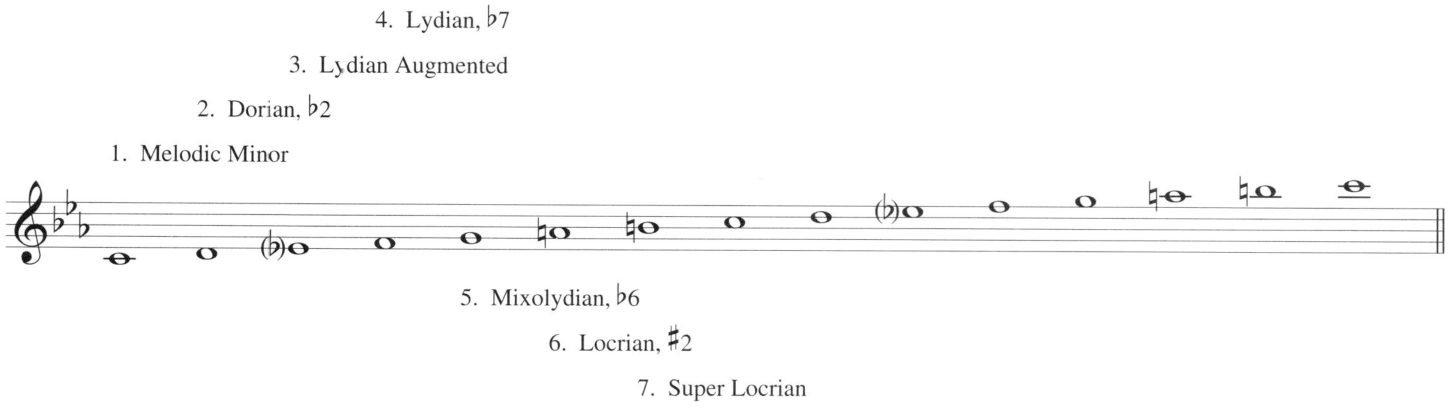

Modal Solo (from *Live at the Green Mill*)

By Frank Catalano

gliss. notes
Fm7
gliss. notes
Em7
8va

Modal Etude/Study

MUSIC GLOSSARY

Accent: To emphasize a note so that it stands out.

Accidental: A note whose pitch is not part of the scale or key signature.

Altissimo: Very high pitched notes.

Arpeggio: Notes of a chord that are played in sequence.

Bar: Another name for a measure.

Beat: The pulse of the music. In 3/4 time, there are three quarter-note beats per measure.

Bend: A jazz term where you slide a note up or down in pitch.

Cadenza: An unaccompanied solo section, usually used to let the soloist show their chops.

Chart: Written arrangement of a song.

Chops: Jazz term for technical facility.

Coda: Closing section in a musical work usually marked with a coda sign.

Cut-Time: Same as 2/2 time.

Da Capo: From the "head" or beginning.

Dal Segno: From the D.S. sign.

Dissonance: Unresolved or clashing notes. There are various levels. I like music that contains dissonance because I feel like it has more ebb and flow or movement.

Doit: Jazz term referring to a note that slides upwards chromatically to an indefinite pitch.

Dolce: Sweetly.

Double-Time: The music, including chord progression, becomes twice as fast as the original tempo.

Double-Time Feel: Phrases occur twice as fast original tempo, but the original length of the chord progression does not change.

Downbeat: First beat of a measure. Sometimes used to describe beats 1, 2, 3, 4 in 4/4 time when eighth notes are present.

Down-Tempo Slow: Moody music. Also an electronic music genre.

Fall: Playing a note and then forcing the pitch of that note to drop.

Fill: A jazz or rock term where a musician improvises for a short time between designated measures.

Fine: The end of the song (pronounced "FEE-nay").

Flam: A drum beat in which both sticks strike the head almost simultaneously but are heard to do so separately. Can also mean two instruments that are supposed to be playing together but are heard slightly apart.

Flat: 1) A pitch is lower than it should be;
2) A flat symbol that means a note should be lowered by a half step.

Forte: Strong or Loud.

Grace Note: A note added as an embellishment.

Head: Melody of a song.

Intro: Opening section.

Jazz Standard: A well-known song from jazz repertoire.

Legato: Played smoothly in a connected manner.

Measure: A bar. In 4/4 time, a measure is four quarter notes in length.

Medley: Musical piece that contains excerpts from several musical pieces.

Melody: The main theme of a song.

Modulation: When a musical piece changes keys, often designated by a key signature change.

Natural: A symbol that cancels the effect of a sharp sign or flat sign.

Octave: 12 half steps (or semitones) make up an octave.

Organ Trio: A classic jazz organ group usually consisting of a Hammond B3 organ, drums, and either a guitar or saxophone.

Pianissimo: Very soft and gentle, low volume.

Presto: Very quickly.

Quartal: Music based on 4th intervals.

Reprise: Repeat or return to main theme.

Semitone: Smallest pitch difference, a half step in Western music, e.g., C to C♯.

Sharp: A symbol that raises the pitch of a note by a half step or semitone.

Straight-Eighths: Even eighth notes that do not have a swing feel.

Swing: Musical term where the eighth note on the beat is longer and the offbeat eighth note is shorter.

Syncopation: The displacement of the usual rhythmic accent away from a strong beat onto a weak beat.

Tacet: Do not play.

Tempo: Time, the overall speed of a song.

Tessitura: Most comfortable pitch range of an instrument or vocalist.

Timbre: The quality of a musical tone.

Time: The speed of a song, the time signature in which the song is to be performed.

Top: Beginning of the song.

Un poco: A little bit.

Up-Tempo: Music with a fast pace.

Vibrato: Repeated slight variation in the pitch of a note, used as a means of expression.

ONLINE VIDEOS

Quick Tips – Advanced Saxophone Lessons

Time

Embouchure

Reed Placement

Soprano Style

Long Tones

Altissimo

Vowels

Split-Tones

Sub-Tones

Wrist Placement

Bis Key and Adolphe

False Fingerings

Reverse Keys

Pop Fingerings

Enclosures

Exercises

In the Band – Studio Play-Along Session

Tuna Town

Bang

F Blues

Rhythm Changes

Up-Tempo Modal Study

Tetrachord Study

ACKNOWLEDGMENTS

A huge thanks to Jeff Schroedl, Larry Morton, and everyone at Hal Leonard Corporation for asking me to write this book; everyone involved in making the online video: legendary Smashing Pumpkin and Grammy-winning drummer Jimmy Chamberlin, bassist Emma Dayhuff, pianist Scott Williams, engineer Dan Steinman, and videographer Mark Nadolski; my endorsers: Yamaha, D'Addario Woodwinds, and JodyJazz for making sure I have awesome equipment to perform on; artist Eric Nietzer for doing the illustrations; pianist Jim Holman for contributing to this book; and my amazing wife Sona Tazian for editing this book.

Much gratitude to: Jim, Janet, Rob, Gina, John, Mike, and Susan D'Addario, Kristen McKeon, Chris Scialfa, Jody Espina, John Wittmann, Jennifer Veirling, Jalissa Gaucho, Rory Mazzela, Roger Eaton, Jeff Peterson, Randy Brecker, David Sanborn, Von Freeman, Josh Sherman, Jason Koransky, Rick Drumm, Rob Polan, Jarod Bufe, Dick Robertson, Mark Bettcher, Greg Wojcik, Ted Nash, Paul Mertens, Larry Novak, Bob Devos, Pete Christlieb, Eric Alexander, Louis Marks and the Ropeadope family, Mike and Christine Jeffers, Michelle Amore, IV Lab Studios, Damian Gress, Robert Gay, Tom Wiedrich, Chicago Hand Surgery Center, Mark Overton, Lee Mendelson, Ramon Esparza, Pete Biedron, and my Mom and entire family.

ABOUT THE AUTHOR

"Frank Catalano is John Coltrane energy for the 21st century." – *Downbeat* magazine

At the time of this writing, Frank Catalano's most recent recording, *Love Supreme Collective*, was the No. 1 seller on the iTunes jazz charts. Catalano's *Bang!* and *Mighty Burner* recordings for the legendary Savoy Label both topped the Billboard sales charts, with *Mighty Burner* dominating the Billboard Charts for 20 straight weeks, making it an international best seller.

Catalano's genre-bending style can be heard on numerous Grammy-winning and Platinum-selling recordings. He has performed with a "who's who" list of legends including Elvin Jones, Betty Carter, Louie Bellson, Miles Davis, Les Claypool, Carlos Santana, Tony Bennett, Beyoncé, Destiny's Child, Jennifer Lopez, John Legend, Johnny Hammond Smith, Charles Earland, Seal, Clark Terry, Barrett Deems, Randy Brecker, Ira Sullivan, Cyrille Neville, Curtis Mayfield, Junior Wells, Von Freeman, Buddy Defranco, and many others. Catalano's solo career began as a teenager when he was signed to the iconic Delmark label. He is currently signed to Ropeadope Records and is recording his next project with Jimmy Chamberlin of Smashing Pumpkins fame.

Catalano has presented over 500 clinics/master classes and endorses Yamaha, D'Addario Woodwind and JodyJazz products. According to the *New York Times*, Catalano has one of the world's largest and most valuable vintage saxophone collections. He is also a patented inventor and holds a Bachelor of Arts degree in Classical Composition from DePaul University. For more information, check out his website: *www.catalanomusic.com*.

HAL•LEONARD®

SAXOPHONE PLAY-ALONG

The Saxophone Play-Along Series will help you play your favorite songs quickly and easily. Just follow the music, listen to the audio to hear how the saxophone should sound, and then play along using the separate backing tracks. Each song is printed twice in the book: once for alto and once for tenor saxes. The melody and lyrics are also included. The audio CD is playable on any CD player but it can also be used in your computer to adjust the recording to any tempo without changing pitch! Books with online audio also include **PLAYBACK+** *options such as looping and tempo adjustments.*

1. ROCK 'N' ROLL

Bony Moronie • Charlie Brown • Hand Clappin' • Honky Tonk (Parts 1 & 2) • I'm Walkin' • Lucille (You Won't Do Your Daddy's Will) • See You Later, Alligator • Shake, Rattle and Roll.

00113137 Book/CD Pack...$16.99

2. R&B

Cleo's Mood • I Got a Woman • Pick up the Pieces • Respect • Shot Gun • Soul Finger • Soul Serenade • Unchain My Heart.

00113177 Book/CD Pack...$16.99

3. CLASSIC ROCK

Baker Street • Deacon Blues • The Heart of Rock and Roll • Jazzman • Smooth Operator • Turn the Page • Who Can It Be Now? • Young Americans.

00113429 Book/CD Pack...$16.99

4. SAX CLASSICS

Boulevard of Broken Dreams • Harlem Nocturne • Night Train • Peter Gunn • The Pink Panther • St. Thomas • Tequila • Yakety Sax.

00114393 Book/Online Audio. $16.99

5. CHARLIE PARKER

Billie's Bounce (Bill's Bounce) • Confirmation • Dewey Square • Donna Lee • Now's the Time • Ornithology • Scrapple from the Apple • Yardbird Suite.

00118286 Book/Online Audio..$16.99

6. DAVE KOZ

All I See Is You • Can't Let You Go (The Sha La Song) • Emily • Honey-Dipped • Know You by Heart • Put the Top Down • Together Again • You Make Me Smile.

00118292 Book/Online Audio $16.99

7. GROVER WASHINGTON, JR.

East River Drive • Just the Two of Us • Let It Flow • Make Me a Memory (Sad Samba) • Mr. Magic • Take Five • Take Me There • Winelight.

00118293 Book/Online Audio $16.99

8. DAVID SANBORN

Anything You Want • Bang Bang • Chicago Song • Comin' Home Baby • The Dream • Hideaway • Slam • Straight to the Heart.

00125694 Book/CD Pack...$16.99

9. CHRISTMAS

The Christmas Song (Chestnuts Roasting on an Open Fire) • Christmas Time Is Here • Count Your Blessings Instead of Sheep • Do You Hear What I Hear • Have Yourself a Merry Little Christmas • The Little Drummer Boy • White Christmas • Winter Wonderland.

00148170 Book/Online Audio $16.99

HAL•LEONARD® CORPORATION

7777 W. Bluemound Rd. P.O. Box 13819 Milwaukee, WI 53213

Visit Hal Leonard online at **www.halleonard.com**